W9-BWL-937

CASE STUDIES IN

CULTURAL ANTHROPOLOGY

GENERAL EDITORS

George and Louise Spindler

STANFORD UNIVERSITY

FISHERMEN OF SOUTH THAILAND

The Malay Villagers

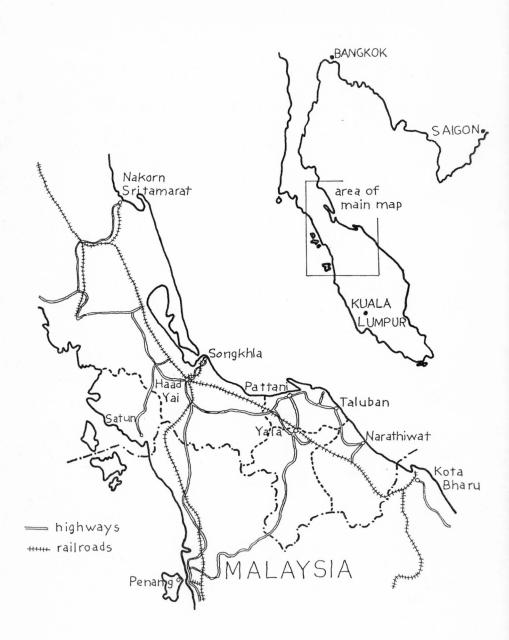

THE LIBRARY
ST. MARY'S COLLEGE OF MARYLAND
ST. MARY'S CITY, MARYLAND 20686

FISHERMEN OF
SOUTH THAILAND
The Malay Villagers

By

THOMAS M. FRASER, JR.

University of Massachusetts

HOLT, RINEHART AND WINSTON, INC.

NEW YORK   CHICAGO   SAN FRANCISCO   TORONTO   LONDON

THE LIBRARY
ST MARY'S COLLEGE OF MARYLAND
ST. MARY'S CITY, MARYLAND 20686

Illustration on cover is of a village elder, Pak Sa, *salvaging string from an old cotton net.*

Copyright © 1966 by Holt, Rinehart and Winston, Inc.
All rights reserved
Library of Congress Catalogue Card Number: 66-18803

22912–0116

Printed in the United States of America

Foreword

About the Series

These case studies in cultural anthropology are designed to bring to students, in beginning and intermediate courses in the social sciences, insights into the richness and complexity of human life as it is lived in different ways and in different places. They are written by men and women who have lived in the societies they write about, and who are professionally trained as observers and interpreters of human behavior. The authors are also teachers, and in writing their books they have kept the students who will read them foremost in their minds. It is our belief that when an understanding of ways of life very different from one's own is gained, abstractions and generalizations about social structure, cultural values, subsistence techniques, and the other universal categories of human social behavior become meaningful.

About the Author

Thomas M. Fraser, Jr., is assistant professor of anthropology at the University of Massachusetts. He studied at Harvard, the University of New Mexico, and received his doctorate from Columbia University. He has done fieldwork among the Pueblo Indians of New Mexico (1951), in India (1958–1960), and East Africa (1965), in addition to his studies of the Malays of South Thailand (1956, 1960, 1964). He is author of *Rusembilan, A Malay Fishing Village in Southern Thailand,* as well as a number of articles in scholarly journals dealing with cultural change and applied anthropology in South Asia. He is currently preparing a book-length study on directed cultural change in India, and is helping develop a program of applied anthropological research in Uganda.

About the Book

This is a case study of the people of Rusembilan. They are Muslims and in this and other features are set off from the rest of Thailand in a cultural area oriented toward Malaysia. In this case study Thomas Fraser provides not only a description of a most interesting people and their culture, but also stimulating intellectual fare in the analytic exploration of significant internal relationships in the social, economic, and ecological adaptations they have made and are making.

The author shows how the organization of the boat crews manning the *koleks* setting off each day for offshore fishing is intimately linked with the network of social relationships and of communication in the village, as well as economic affairs and subsistence.

He also gives us a very clear analysis of the compartmentalization of values in this culture resulting from the influence of Islam superimposed on a traditional Malay, Southeast Asian culture of long standing, which in turn is influenced by Thai culture through the efforts of the government of Thailand. In view of this compartmentalization, it is surprising that the people of Rusembilan have managed to create and maintain a satisfying and apparently well-organized way of life.

But this way of life is showing signs of change. The internal integration of the village is declining in significant degree due to the substitution of outboard motors for oars and sails on the *koleks,* and the use of nylon, rather than cotton nets for fishing. These seemingly minor technical substitutions have directly affected the allocation of roles and statuses in the community, and the flow of communication. The analysis demonstrates how delicately poised cultural systems may be, and how relatively minor changes may cause basic shifts in the whole system.

This case study also presents the more esoteric aspects of the culture of Rusembilan. Dr. Fraser describes the spiritual forces surrounding the people, and the incantations, trances, spirit possession, seances, and divinations they use to control these forces, propitiate them, and predict their behavior. Here again one sees the traditional Malaysian culture operating under the relatively superficial imposition of Islamic elements. Thus one can see public seances where spirits are given the opportunity to put on a play, through their mediums, in the same community where nearly every adult can recite the Koran in its entirety, though very few understand the meaning of what they are reciting.

George and Louise Spindler
General Editors

Stanford, California
February 1966

Acknowledgments

I owe a special debt of gratitude to the villagers of Rusembilan who have borne so good-naturedly my presence in their village and investigation into their lives on three separate occasions. I am also deeply indebted to Haji Mohamed Abdul Kadir, who assisted me in 1956, and the Chanya Withan Marohabutra (Wan Jussof), who assisted me in 1964, for their help with information, linguistic problems, and for the tact and understanding they displayed in situations made embarrassing through differences in culture.

I wish to thank Cornell University Press for allowing me to use material published in my book, *Rusembilan, A Malay Fishing Village in Southern Thailand* (1960), and for permission to quote passages on pages 27, 60–61, and 86.

Also, my thanks are due to the Asian and African Studies Program of Amherst, Mount Holyoke, and Smith Colleges, and to the University of Massachusetts for a grant enabling me to spend the summer of 1964 in Rusembilan and also for a Faculty Growth Grant which has allowed me to devote my full time during the summer of 1965 to preparing this manuscript.

THOMAS M. FRASER, JR.

University of Massachusetts
Amherst, Massachusetts
February 1966

Contents

Foreword   vii

Acknowledgments   ix

1. The Village and Its Context   1

2. Making a Living   8

     The Yearly Cycle of Fishing and Rice Cultivation, 8
     Plantations in a Cash Economy, 16
     Economic Specialists and the Market Town, 20

3. The Web of Life   26

     The Family and Household, 26
     The Kampong: *Neighbors and Kinsmen, 32*
     The Region: Kin and Ceremonial Networks, 36

4. Maintaining Control   40

     The "Good Man" and His Influence, 40
     The Tambon *and the Village Headman, 45*
     District, Changwat, *and Nation, 49*

5. Dealing with the Supernatural   56

     Spirits, Illness, and the Bomo, *56*
     Fasts, Feasts, and the Imam, 63
     Religion and the Crises of Life, 69

6. Learning to Live in Rusembilan   75

     Basic Values and Early Training, 75
     Education: Informal, Formal, and National, 80
     Adult Status: A Resolution of Contradictions, 86

7. The Changing Scene   90

    Technological Change and Community Integration, 90
    Economic Change: From Sea to Jungle, 94
    The Government and Planned Change, 97
    Minority Groups and National Security, 100

Glossary   106

References Cited   109

Recommended Reading   109

A kolek *being launched from its beach shed by crew members. Boats are beached during periods of bright moonlight when fishing is impossible.*

Preparation of mutton curry to be served with rice and condiments at a makan pulot.

View of Rusembilan from harvested padi *fields behind the village. Cattle, guarded by young boy, and sheep graze on dead stalks.*

The bomo *incants over a plate of offerings for spirits while a village dancer performs the first stages of the* silat.

Stern of kolek *equipped with "long-tail" outboard motor. Ornate crutch once held its mast when not in use. Garland of flowers is to please sea spirits.*

A group of women playing a low-stakes lottery game, introduced at Rusembilan by the woman in the center.

FISHERMEN OF SOUTH THAILAND

The Malay Villagers

1

The Village and Its Context

LEGEND TELLS of a Chinese princess, traveling with her brother and retinue through the tributary states of Southeast Asia. So entrancing was the beauty, and so charming the people of the kingdom of Pattani, that the young brother determined to remain in the kingdom and embrace the local faith. When the princess found that her pleas could not deter the resolve of the young prince, she took her own life rather than returning in shame to China. Shortly after her funeral, nine members of the retinue set sail to inform the Emperor of these sad events, but hardly had they left Pattani's harbor than accident befell them, and all drowned. The loyal Chinese residents of the kingdom erected a temple in the town of Pattani to commemorate their princess, and near the site of the shipwreck they planted nine pine trees, one for each of the members of the party that had hoped to return to China. It is on this site, according to tradition, that the present village of Rusembilan stands. The name of the village is taken from the two Malay words, *sembilan,* meaning "nine," and *ru,* meaning "casuarina," the local species of pine tree.

Rusembilan is a village of slightly over 1000 inhabitants, located on the shore of the Gulf of Thailand, about $3\frac{1}{2}$ miles from the provincial capital of Pattani. Like the great majority of villages in the four southern provinces of Thailand (Pattani, Yala, Narathiwat, and Satun), Rusembilan is a village of Malay people. Its residents speak the Malay language, very few of them being able to speak (let alone read or write) the national language of Thailand. They are Muslims, although the rest of Thailand is Buddhist. Their culture is typically Malay, its affiliations reaching to the south in peninsular Malaysia rather than north into Thailand.

Malay culture has deep and important roots in the region that is now South Thailand. During the fourteenth century, the Malay kingdom of Pattani, comprising the present four Malay-speaking provinces of Thailand as well as additional territory to the north, ranked as one of the largest and most important kingdoms of the entire Malayan Peninsula. Although the history dates from

before the introduction of Islam to the peninsula, much of the stature and importance of Pattani stemmed from its development as a center of Islamic schol-
arship and tradition (a feature which to some extent still characterizes it today).
The period of Pattani's florescence as an economic, religious, and cultural center
was long-lived, extending (with only minor set-backs) over the reign of eighteen sultans and sultanas belonging to two major dynasties before finally bowing
to invasion by the Siamese (Thai) in 1832.

Shortly after they had gained control of the west coast port city of Malacca in 1511, the Portuguese were granted trading rights in Pattani on the east
coast. However, their full attention seems to have been required in Malacca, for
they did little to exploit or develop the trade of the east coast—in fact, it is reported that they burned the town of Pattani in 1523. European trade with Pattani was sporadic until the beginning of the seventeenth century when the Dutch
were given permission by the sultana to establish a "factory," or resident trade
warehouse, in Pattani. This was promptly burned down by rival British trading
interests. In 1612, both the British and Dutch had flourishing factories in the
town of Pattani. Because of struggles elsewhere in Southeast Asia between the
expanding trade empires of Britain and the Netherlands, both of these factories
were abandoned some time after 1622 and European trade never again played
an important part in Pattani's history. As Siam to the north and several of the
Malay states to the south became more powerful and economically important
with the infusion of European mercantile and diplomatic advice and control,
Pattani began to be eclipsed from the interregional scene, an eclipse that did not
become total until ultimate defeat by the Siamese in 1832. In brief, this is the
historical background of the Malay area of South Thailand. It represents a past
which is by no means forgotten and a tradition which lives vigorously on both
sides of a recently contrived international frontier.

In the area under consideration, the east coast of the peninsula makes
one of its characteristic jogs to the westward, like a stair step. These steps are
the result of alluvial depositions from the major north-flowing rivers. In this case
the Pattani River flows from the high tin-bearing hills along the Malayan border
in a generally northward direction through Yala and Pattani provinces to its
deltaic mouths in the districts surrounding the town of Pattani. The east-facing
coast of Pattani province and all of Narathiwat has broad sandy beaches open to
the surf of the Gulf of Thailand and the South China Sea. This type of coast is
characteristic of most of the coastline of the Malaysian states of Kelantan and
Trengganu to the south. Beyond the beach are either low marshy swamplands
(as in Narathiwat) or low sedimentary ranges (as in east coast Pattani). The
north-facing coast along the remainder of Pattani province and into the neighboring province of Songkhla, protected from the scouring action of the sea by
the range of hills mentioned above and their trailing sand-dune cape, is composed of alluvial mud. While this mud presents certain problems to the fishing
villages situated there, the north coast has the definite advantage of affording far
greater protection from both wind and sea, and is therefore more heavily populated than the otherwise more convenient and more beautiful beaches of the
east. Inland from the north coast the land very gradually slopes upward for

some 25 miles before reaching the foothills of the jungle-covered mountains of central and southern Yala province. This alluvial land, much of it within the delta system of the Pattani River, provides the most productive rice growing land in the three-province area. Coconuts grow in abundance along the sandy stretches behind the beaches of both the east and north coasts. Land for rubber and fruit growing, as well as occasional upland dry rice fields (swiddens), is constantly being cleared in the mountainous areas south of Yala town and in the portions of Songkhla province immediately to the west of Pattani province.

South Thailand, situated between about 6° and 10° north of the equator enjoys a typical tropical climate. Mean annual temperature is 80° F with only about a two-degree seasonal variation; in fact daily variations are always greater than seasonal variations. There is a clearly defined rainy season brought by the northeast monsoon beginning in the middle of October and lasting through the middle of January. During this three-month period more than half of the annual rainfull occurs. Rainfall is not absent during the other months of the year, however, averaging about 5 inches a month during the "dry season." Throughout the year the coastal areas are cooled by breezes, generally toward the sea during the day and onshore at night. During the monsoon season wind velocities increase, causing high seas and inundation of low-lying coastal areas. Because of these wind and sea conditions, most offshore fishing operations completely cease during this period. In Satun and the west coast of the peninsula, rain is brought by the southwest monsoon rather than the northeast monsoon and is confined mainly to the period between June and September. This affords opportunity to Malays of either coast to carry on their traditional occupations throughout the year simply by taking up temporary residence on the opposite coast at the appropriate season.

Satun province, although culturally Malay and religiously Islamic, is in many other respects different from the three Malay-speaking provinces on the east. A far greater proportion of the residents of Satun have learned to use the Thai language and most of their outside contacts are not with the other three provinces from which Satun is isolated by mountainous jungles, but with centers of Thai population in Songkhla, Phattalung, and Haad Yai. Because of its isolation, Satun was never an integral part of the east coast Malay area, although at times it was under the political domination of the Pattani kingdom. Its cultural affinities are with the west coast Malay states of Perlis and Kedah rather than with Kelantan on the east. For these reasons, except when Satun is specifically included, the discussions that follow will be concerned exclusively with Pattani, Yala, and Narathiwat.

Until 1963, these three provinces were linked on land with the rest of Thailand through one point, Khok Pho. This small town on the western fringe of Pattani province is both on the rail line connecting Haad Yai (on the main line between Bangkok and Singapore) with Kota Bharu in Kelantan, and the terminus of a new road opened to general traffic in 1957 leading in from Songkhla province. Although this road provides access to a number of Thai towns in the South, one can still not travel toward Bangkok north of Phuket (on the west) or Nakorn Sritamarat (on the east) except by rail or air. The road does, however, provide good access to the west coast cities of northern Malaya and thence to the rest of peninsular Malaysia. In addition to these road and rail links with Malaysia, another road leads through the heart of Yala province into the Malaysian state of Perak, while innumerable tracks and trails (but no motor roads) lead to both banks of the Golok River separating Narathiwat and Kelantan. There is also a weekly steamer from Bangkok calling at Pattani, Saiburi, and Narathiwat; however, maritime contacts (if not official) are more numerous between this area and Malaya. In 1963 Thai Airways initiated air service three times a week between Bangkok and Pattani, and will in the near future serve Yala. Through train service from the area to Bangkok has also been improved during the past ten years. High priority is being given to highway projects linking the lower half of peninsular Thailand with the capital and to the creation of a new highway link from Songkhla to Pattani. The situation of greater isolation

TABLE 1

POPULATION DATA

Province	Area (km²)	Population (×1000)	Capital-Town (pop.)	Rural (percent)	Muslim (percent)
Pattani	2,013	281.6	16,804	78	78
Yala	4,714	147.3	18,100	71	61
Narathiwat	4,228	266.0	17,631	71	78

Source: Thailand Census, 1960.

from Thailand than from Malaysia, and the efforts of the Thai government to rectify the situation are obvious. The political and economic implications of both will be considered in Chapters 2 and 4 and again in Chapter 7.

The great majority of people in these three provinces are Malays living in villages along the shores, scattered through the alluvial rice lands, and more sparsely in the more rugged rubber-growing interior. Table 1 indicates roughly how this population is distributed throughout the three provinces. Certain important points, however, should be mentioned. The capital towns, in each case bearing the same name as its province, are the only important urban centers in any of these provinces. Narathiwat comes closest to having rival towns in Tanjong Mas, the rail station closest to the capital and also center of a major rice-producing area in the province, and in Sungei Golok, on the frontier of Malaya and center for a large volume of unregulated trade. It is in these centers that the large majority of the non-Malay, or non-Muslim population resides. This urban group is made up of both Thais and Chinese. The later category is difficult to define in Thailand, for the only group recognized as Chinese within the country are actual citizens of China. Even so, there are some 12,000 Chinese in these three provinces, more than half of whom live in Yala. More important, however, are the Thai-born Chinese, citizens of Thailand who are of Chinese descent, culture, language, and religion. From this group come most of the important merchants and shopkeepers. A rough estimate would be that this group makes up half to two thirds of the non-Malay portion of the population. The Thais, except for a relatively few old families in the area, have until recently been government servants on brief assignments in the South, flowing through the area rapidly enough so that few were able to (or wanted to) establish important ties or relationships in the area. At present, as part of the attempt to integrate more closely this area into the Thai nation, a large number of Thai civil servants are being stationed on permanent basis, mostly in the town of Yala. The government has hopes of creating in Yala an important educational, developmental, and administrative center. In Pattani, precisely the same percentage of the population is Muslim as is rural. While this cannot be taken as an equation of individuals, it is indicative of the situation. The higher rural, in relation to Muslim, figure for Yala reflects the Thais and Chinese involved in rubber and tin mining operations in the interior of that province; the opposite situation in Narathiwat reflects the fact that because of its greater isolation from Thailand this province has been more resistant to the influx of urban dwellers, particularly the Thais, from outside.

In terms of economic standards, the South is as well-off as any area in Thailand, and considerably better off than some areas. However, as will be discussed in the final chapter, it is not without its serious economic problems. It is almost exclusively an agricultural and fishing region. Tin, lignite, and small amounts of other minerals including gold have some importance in terms of the national economy, but they have little or no effect on the local peasants either in terms of managerial opportunity, employment, or of locally expendable revenue. By far the most important crops economically are rubber and coconuts, in that order. Even with the recent slump in world rubber prices, and with the inferior processing which most South Thailand rubber is given, the value of rubber produced has surpassed that of all other agricultural and maritime produce combined. A figure somewhere in the neighborhood of a billion *baht* ($50 million) is generally agreed upon for recent years. Coconuts grown for copra, although important for manufacturing within Thailand, do not reach an international market in quantity. While coconuts are of some importance in coastal areas, they are universally overshadowed by fishing or rice growing or both. Local rice production (some 58,000 tons in 1963) is estimated to be sufficient to sustain a population half again as large as that presently in Pattani, Yala, and Narathiwat. Some of this surplus is shipped to Bangkok where it joins the national stock of exportable surplus rice. However, most of it is sold illicitly across the border into Kelantan where, due to a national deficit of rice in Malaysia, prices are considerably higher than in Thailand and Thai export duty can be evaded. Annual yields of fish have fluctuated considerably in recent years, while the price, according to official statistics, has remained nearly constant. In 1954 and again in 1956, over 8000 tons of fish were landed in the Malay provinces of South Thailand. In 1963 the total catch was under 3000 tons. In general, the trend has been in the direction of lower yields each year, a situation noted with grave anxiety among village fishermen. It has, however, provided some incentive for the opening up of rubber-growing lands in the interior of the region. These matters will be discussed in the following chapter.

The main emphasis of the rest of this study will be on a particular fishing village in Pattani province, Rusembilan. This Malay fishing village on the north-facing coast not far from the town of Pattani is typical in large measure of all the fishing villages of the coastal areas of Pattani and Narathiwat. Fishing, the dominant economic activity, has effects on many aspects of the community yet these effects are not sufficiently great to distort the essential quality of Malay village life. For this reason, Rusembilan can be said to be fairly typical, in areas other than economic, of a large number of Malay villages in these three provinces. During the eight-year time span which this study covers, the village of Rusembilan grew in population from 811 persons to 1019 persons. The residents of the village are all Malay Muslims, most of whom have little contact with Thais or Chinese in the nearby provincial capital. During the period under consideration, a number of changes occurred in the village which will be mentioned in the chapters that follow and will be summarized in the final chapter, dealing specifically with change.

Villages such as Rusembilan are a far cry from the traditional anthropological object of study, the isolated tribal group. Proper understanding of these villages must include reference to a far wider field than the community itself. In the chapters that follow, initial attention will be focused on those matters which are most clearly confined to the community, gradually building from there to local interconnections beyond the single village, and finally indicating some of the ways in which the various aspects of village society and culture relate to the broader regional and national scene. To present a model of a coherent, isolable community would be to distort reality. Rusembilan and the many similar village communities in South Thailand are, indeed, peasant communities: they constitute part-societies with part-cultures (Kroeber 1948: 284). They depend for many essential functions on their relationship with complex, national societies, without which they would absolutely lose their characteristic form.

The field work on which this study is based was carried on in the village of Rusembilan and neighboring villages over a period of eight years. The first visit to South Thailand was in 1956, when the author lived for a nine-month period in Rusembilan. This provided the base line from which changes in the society and culture of South Thailand are viewed. A detailed description of Rusembilan and its context, far fuller than can be presented here, is contained in the author's book, *Rusembilan: A Malay Fishing Village in Southern Thailand* (Fraser 1960). In 1960, a two-week visit was paid to Rusembilan and the Pattani area. Again in 1964, the author returned to Rusembilan, this time for two months. During these three visits information was gathered largely through informal discussion with villagers. In the beginning, any information was relevant; later, all that was necessary was to mention a topic and informants would discourse fully on it. An attempt was made to participate as fully as possible in village activities. Actually, the skill and technical specialization involved in fishing made participation in this important area impossible—even as observer, the author sometimes felt decidedly in the way. All village ceremonies and feasts were attended, and many such occasions in other villages were attended in the company of villagers from Rusembilan, affording opportunity to observe the operation of the wide-spreading kin and ceremonial network. Rapport with the villagers was surprisingly easy to establish. The people were pleased and proud that their village had been chosen for study. The presence of a westerner and his wife living within the village was a decided prestige factor in the relations of these people with other Malays and with Thais. Also the presence of the author and his wife proved to be a definite convenience to the villagers in several ways, at least one of which was totally unexpected. It was not surprising that village women were happy to be transported to the Pattani market in the author's Land Rover, nor that the men welcomed transportation to feasts held in other villages. It was somewhat startling, however, to find after some weeks of fieldwork that the location of the author's newly built house with its kerosene pressure lamp shining at night had successfully driven from this previously vacant lot in the village a large number of *hantu,* or malevolent spirits who had formerly plagued villagers passing at night.

In addition to living in the village, observing, discussing, and participating whenever possible, two house-to-house surveys were conducted, one in 1956, the other in 1964. Comparison of these, in addition to providing information on the major events in the lives of almost every resident of Rusembilan, has provided "hard" data on marriage patterns, occupational change, and migrations in and out of the village. The main purpose of the author's field work during the summer of 1964 was to determine what sorts of changes had occurred in Rusembilan and other Malay villages in the area during the eight years since the initial study. It was thought that these changes would have important effects on the whole cultural fabric, and that an understanding of these effects would be important to a general understanding of change in the rural areas of developing nations. While change, an important element in any culture, was the focus of the 1964 study, the present work is not primarily concerned with it. Within the chapters that follow, certain changes that have occurred in Rusembilan will be indicated. This will be done both in the interests of accurate description and, more important, to give a sense of dynamic continuity over time in these Malay fishing villages. The hope is that something of the notion of the community and its relationships with the outside moving along an irreversible stream of time can be captured and conveyed to the reader.

2

Making a Living

The Yearly Cycle of Fishing and Rice Cultivation

FISHING IN THE WATERS of the South China Sea and the Gulf of Thailand is considered to be the only important occupation by the people of Rusembilan even though it is largely a seasonal occupation and directly involves only able-bodied males. Fishing, boats, prices, nets, and other topics related to fishing are uppermost in the minds of members of the community, men, women, and children, at all times. The second most important occupation in these coastal villages is rice cultivation but it is engaged in by many only because it grows during the monsoon season when it is impossible to take the fishing boats out to sea. Because of this preoccupation with fishing, the economies of Rusembilan and other coastal villages are unusually sensitive to fluctuations in the supply of and demand for fish. Objectively, this sensitivity is not necessary, for the east coast area offers opportunity for a wide variety of cash crop production.

The fishing season begins with the retreat of the northeast monsoon and the calming of the sea sometime between the end of December and the middle of February. Although the first two months of the fishing season are usually the most prosperous for the fishing communities, villagers eagerly await the second phase when schools of mackerel begin to be available in accessible waters. During the early period the main catch is *udang ako,* a species of prawn measuring up to 12 inches in length. These prawn are in great demand both in Bangkok and in the Malaysian cities to the south, quantities of them even making their way to canning factories in Japan. The organization of the crew for this type of fishing is essentially the same as that which will be described for the more important mackerel fishing. A major difference, however, is that schools of prawn cannot be located visually, and at least one member of the crew must have a specialized skill in detecting their presence. This is done by diving from the boat, submerging—not necessarily to the bottom—and listening for the sound that the

8

prawns make as they move along the floor of the sea. A skilled diver can detect prawns as much as a mile away, accurately indicating both their direction and distance from the boat.

By the middle of April, reports of the presence of *kembong*, a small species of mackerel, have usually made their way up and down the coast, and much discussion takes place in each village as to the precise day on which the fishermen will first venture forth for this long-awaited catch. The deciding factor in establishing when to launch the *kembong* season, and indeed affecting the fishing routine throughout the season, is the phase of the moon. *Kembong* is netted only at night, for only then can the large schools of fish be detected by the phosphorescent organisms they stir up in the warm waters. The glow in the water can be seen on the horizon for several miles. Obviously, when the moon is shining brightly (and also when the seas are rough) this method of detecting schools of *kembong* becomes extremely difficult and the fishermen remain ashore.

The boats, *perahu kolek*, used for both *kembong* and *udang ako* fishing represent the most important possessions of the villagers—both socially and economically. There are relatively few of these boats in a village such as Rusembilan: twelve in 1956 and fourteen in 1964; however, only eight of this number represented a continuity of ownership. These *kolek*, ranging from 35 to over 50 feet in length, are carefully maintained, as they represent an investment of some 15,000 *baht* ($750). At least once every two or three years they are freshly painted with long brilliant stripes. The high, slender bows are further decorated with floral designs or traditional Islamic motifs. Each time a boat returns from fishing it is thoroughly washed by a member of the crew specifically assigned to this task. Most of these elegant *kolek* are owned by individuals, occasionally jointly by two; and these men are among the group of informal leaders of the village to be discussed in Chapter 4. Two *kolek* in Rusembilan are owned cooperatively by their crew members.

Before the start of the prawn fishing season, the boat crew is assembled. Recruiting, as indeed all decision-making authority, is in the hands of the steerer. While the steerer may also be owner of the boat, or the owner's son, this is not necessarily the case. It is essential, however, that he be a skillful and experienced fisherman, with a knack not only of knowing where the schools of fish are apt to be, but also for assessing offshore sea and weather conditions. In recruiting crew members, the steerer attempts to find and attract village fishermen with the greatest amount of skill and experience themselves. Potential crew members, for their part, attempt to join with boats and steerers who have demonstrated their "luck" in previous seasons. It is apparent, therefore, that in this freely competitive situation, the reputation of a boat and its steerer is quickly established and rather difficult to change. The cooperative boats are at a relative disadvantage in this competition, as the crew members have a financial stake in their boats, making mobility a more serious and difficult matter—there is a feeling among villagers that crews of these boats are made up of fishermen who could not get positions on the better boats.

In addition to the steerer and the crew member responsible for washing the *kolek* after use, there are two other specialists on the boat crew. These are the chief net handlers, who under the direction of the steerer are responsible for the proper setting and recovery of the large gill net used for *kembong*. Before motorization of the fishing fleets of coastal South Thailand, these men handled the bow paddles, assisting the steerer in maneuvering the boat quickly and efficiently while it was encircling a school of fish. Other members of the crew do not perform specialized roles. In the past their importance lay largely in providing oar power when winds were not favorable for sailing; today almost their only function is in handling the *kembong* nets. A problem has arisen with this change of roles which will be dealt with more fully in Chapter 7: while crews of thirteen or fifteen were necessary before motorization in order to propel the *kolek,* from five to seven men can easily handle the nylon nets which are in use today. However, to avoid underemployment in the fishing villages, *kolek* still go to sea with large crews—eleven men was the smallest crew in Rusembilan in 1964. Not only is there under-utilization of manpower aboard the boats, and occasionally even interference with the work of others, but the feeling exists among some of the fishermen that they (whose services are more essential) are in effect subsidizing other villagers who are not "carrying their own weight."

When moonlight is no problem, fishermen prefer to set out for the fishing grounds in the late afternoon and are thus able to drop their nets as soon as darkness falls. The probability is that they will then be able to fill their boats and return to shore earlier to benefit from the better market prices in the early morning. However, if the moon is high in the sky in the early evening, the evening's launching must be postponed. Prior to motorization, the *kolek* along the east coast either sailed or paddled (depending on the orientation of the coast line to the prevailing winds) to the fishing grounds. From the Rusembilan beach which faces north, sailing was generally possible. The return trip often involved paddling. Today, all the boats use outboard motors; neither sails nor paddles are taken to sea. Every crew member on a boat must provide two nets, each approximately 40 by 60 feet. Traditionally these were cotton and made in the villages, but now they are of nylon and are purchased from large towns such as Pattani. These nets are sewn together so that they form a continuous ribbon 40 feet deep and from a quarter to a third of a mile long. When a school of fish is sighted, the *kolek* approaches at full speed and one end of the net with an attached marking buoy is dropped. The boat then races in a circle as the net is paid out until the two ends meet, encircling the school of fish. Immediately the crew members begin shouting, beating the water with special convex poles, and playing a magneto-operated spotlight (previously kerosene flares) over the area encompassed by the net. The noise and light effectively disperse the school of mackerel and the fleeing fish become enmeshed in the gill net which is then hauled into the boat, steadily decreasing the circumference of the circle. Except for the last netting of the night's operations, hundreds of fish must be disentangled from the nets as they are hauled into the boat, or, if the catch is unusually large (1000-2000), removal of the fish may be accomplished after the whole net has been brought into the boat. This work requires skill and speed. It is made more difficult by a number of fish inevitably getting underfoot instead of under the deck planks where they are to be stored, and in addition, this is when most fishing accidents occur, including wounds from small sharks brought in with the catch, and more serious, the fatal bites of sea snakes inadvertently landed.

When the *kolek* is loaded to capacity, or when the steerer feels that further netting is not worth the effort, the boat returns home where the fish will be unloaded and distributed by the wives (or mothers) of the crew. Except for the crewman responsible for washing the boat, the responsibility of the men ceases as soon as they reach shore. In the past, when cotton nets were used, the whole crew had the arduous task of removing the net from the *kolek* and

TABLE 2

DISTRIBUTION OF FISH

	1956 Bagian Ketchil (14-man crew)		1964 Bagian Besar (12-man crew)	
	Share	Total	Share	Total
Per man	1	14	$\frac{1}{2}$	6
Per net	$\frac{1}{2}$	14	$\frac{1}{4}$	6
Steerer	1	1	$\frac{1}{2}$	$\frac{1}{2}$
Washer	$\frac{1}{2}$	$\frac{1}{2}$	$\frac{1}{4}$	$\frac{1}{4}$
Net man	$\frac{1}{2}$	2	$\frac{1}{4}$	1
Boat	$1\frac{1}{2}$	$1\frac{1}{2}$	1	1
Engine			$3\frac{1}{4}$	$3\frac{1}{4}$
Total		33		18

stretching it on racks along the beach to dry; the nylon net is simply left within the boat.

Distribution of fish follows a consistent pattern for each *kolek*. While there are differences in details of distribution among almost all of the boats at Rusembilan, there are essentially only two broad patterns, *bagian besar* and *bagian ketchil,* large and small shares, respectively. In the *bagian ketchil,* fish are divided into twice as many piles, or shares, as in the *bagian besar.* This requires a larger space on the beach for sorting, but it somewhat simplifies the handling of small payments (fractional shares) for specialized services of some of the crew members. Table 2 indicates typical distribution of shares of both types. With the introduction of tow boats at Rusembilan in the middle of the *kembong* season in 1956, groups of three *kolek* would pool their distribution of fish. It was quickly found that using the *bagian ketchil* the space required for the hundred-odd piles of fish was simply not available. Even though the use of tow boats was short-lived, and by the next season all *kolek* had acquired individual outboard motors (see Chapter 7), the pattern of large shares continued to be used by most of the crews.

After the fish have been divided into the proper number of shares, each woman, representing one of the crew members, collects in her basket the number of shares due her. From this a few fish are taken to meet her family's needs for the day; these are usually given to a child to be taken directly home. Only if the catch has been unusually small will several women pool their shares for common marketing. Otherwise, each woman from Rusembilan takes her own basket and, traditionally, carries it on her head the 3½ miles into the market in Pattani. Since the establishment of regular bus service from Rusembilan to Pattani, almost no one walks, preferring to pay the fare of 2 *baht* (10 cents) plus 1 *baht* for a basket of fish. Not only is it less tiring to ride the bus than to walk, but it gains the women almost an hour in getting to the market where prices often start to drop rapidly after 8:00 A.M. It is misleading to speak of average number of fish or of average market price; both figures fluctuate widely. The size of the catch (always expressed in terms of the size of the share) varies from a relatively frequent zero up to a maximum of about three hundred fish per large share (that is, the number of fish due to an ordinary crewman's family). An average catch, in the sense that it is expected and elicits neither disappointment nor excitement, would be about one hundred fish per share. Market price for *kembong* varies directly with supply, the demand for this species in the area being constant. Only in cases of serious oversupply is any attempt made to export *kembong* out of the east coast provinces; importation from the west coast to meet local demand is becoming more usual. The range of prices in 1956 was between 50 and 200 *baht* ($2.50–$10.00) per hundred *kembong*, 100 *baht* ($5.00) per hundred was a reasonable and fairly common price. By 1964 the whole range had slipped downward with an "average" between 40 and 60 *baht* ($2.00–$3.00) per hundred, and the season's top price rising to only 120 *baht*.

In general, village women sell their fish directly to one of four Chinese fish dealers. The prices they get from these dealers are not quite as good as they would be able to get in the open market; however, here they are able to sell their whole load at once rather than piecemeal at retail. If the catch is unusually small, the somewhat higher retail price may induce a woman to establish herself outside of the municipal market and sell her fish directly to consumers. In the case of *kembong*, the dealer packs small quantities in ice and channels them into the local distribution network which he controls. This consists of a fleet of trucks, motorcycles, and bicycles which fans out from Pattani to the interior districts of the provinces of Pattani, Yala, and Narathiwat. Other species of fish handled by the Chinese dealers are distributed in bulk either to Bangkok or Penang. This will be discussed briefly at the end of this chapter.

Although *kembong* and the large prawns account for the great majority of maritime economic resources in coastal villages such as Rusembilan, they are by no means the only maritime activities. Those men who are unable to secure a position with a *kolek* crew (and with the reduction in required crew size and the increase of village population, this is an increasing number of men) and most village men during times when it is impossible to fish for mackerel or prawns, fish for the many species of small fish which live in the shallow waters near the shore. Older men, who no longer have the strength to carry on the long hard hours of *kembong* fishing, often retire to a life of crab netting along with their wives and other members of their family who may be available. These minor fishing activities involve a number of different net types and techniques. Most also require the use of a small, one- or two-man boat. Such boats are inexpensive and most families in coastal villages own one. Many of the larger of these now are equipped with their own outboard motors. However, the lavish care and decoration characteristic of the *kolek* is totally absent among these smaller boats: it is sufficient that they do not leak so badly that they founder.

Except for crabs and *udang belachan*, a miniature shrimp which is ground and fermented in brine to produce a paste used by Thais and Malays alike, the yields of minor fishing activities rarely reach the market. They can be consumed by the family of the fisherman, or if a surplus is caught, sharing with neighbors is common. Crabs are sold at retail by the fisherman's wife, as there is no external or organized local market for them. *Udang belachan* are sometimes sold to Chinese dealers and sometimes processed in the village where the added trouble of alternate salting and drying and steeping results in significantly higher prices.

After the fishing season is over on the east coast, there are usually a number of men, not owning rice land, who travel to the west coast to take advantage of the differently timed fishing season there. Occasionally, they may be able to get into Malaysia where fish prices in the urban centers tend to be higher than in Thailand. Usually, however, they settle temporarily in Satun where they feel less out of place than they would in a non-Muslim province. But because many of the Malays in Satun can converse in Thai, and because their dialect of Malay is different from the east coast Malay, the men from east coast villages try to form their own boat crews before setting out to Satun. In Rusembilan, it is usually the crews of the cooperative *kolek* who take advantage of this opportunity. They travel to Satun as a group, settle in a village where one or more of them has friends or connections (living in hastily constructed bamboo and thatch huts) and rent a boat for the season. As they do not ordinarily take their wives with them, the men must share the responsibility of marketing the catch, which is a task they do not view with much pleasure, particularly as all market transactions in this area are conducted in the Thai language. This practice has been declining in recent years as the opportunity for hire-tapping in the east coast provinces has been increasing.[1] In this occupation, coastal villagers not only feel more at home with the people of the inland villages, but they ordinarily finish the season with considerably more cash.

The staple food throughout Southeast Asia is, of course, rice. Its importance is reflected in the Malay expression for "to have a meal," *makan nasi* (eat rice). Although fishing looms as the most important and exciting economic activity in Rusembilan and other coastal villages, the cultivation of rice is not neglected. Roughly three quarters of Rusembilan families own flooded *padi* (unprocessed, uncooked rice) fields beyond the village borders or they work on the

---

[1] The practice of tapping rubber on the estates of others. Payment is usually 50 percent of the tapper's yield.

fields of nonresident owners either on a share-crop arrangement or for a small yearly rental. Before 1950, Rusembilan managed to produce sufficient rice to meet its own needs. Since then, however, due to increasing salinization of some of the fields, increase in population, and the fact that these fishermen have no overwhelming interest in rice cultivation, the coastal villages have come more and more to depend on rice grown in the interior and purchased in the market to fill their dietary needs. Perhaps the most important reason that rice continues to be cultivated at all in these fishing villages is that the rains required to flood the rice fields occur with the northeast monsoon when the seas are too rough for any large-scale fishing.

The first plowing of the *padi* fields is begun in July or August by men during the period of the full moon when nighttime fishing is temporarily halted. A heavy plow, *nanga,* pulled usually by one bullock, is required to break the dry and sun-caked soil. This operation may take a cultivator from two days to a week, as he works only during the early morning and late evening hours when the heat is less intense. Large landholders like to stagger the initial plowing of their fields so that subsequent operations will not all fall at the same time. Heavy plowing is followed by raking with the *gurah,* also pulled by a bullock, to break up the largest clods left from the plowing. Raking can usually be accomplished in one morning. The fields are now ready for seeding, which simply involves broadcasting rice saved from the previous year's harvest over a selected seeding area or field (no more than a quarter of an individual's total holding). Until after the rains have started, and fishing stopped, this is all that is done. Many well-to-do families own one plowing bullock; others rent them from men who own several. This is the only period of the year during which such cattle are used.

By October, but continuing on into November, after sufficient rain has fallen to cover the rice fields and the seedlings have grown to a height of between 4 and 6 inches, one of the two periods of intensive activity in the rice cycle begins, transplantation. Broadcasting the seed and transplanting are done by both sexes. For transplanting, it is desirable to assemble a group of a dozen or more people. Unlike most activities in Rusembilan, recruitment of groups to work in the rice fields is not on the basis of association among members of the same boat crew, but on the basis of kinship proximity. A man will first call on his own and his wife's closest relatives living in the village, then the next closest degree of relatives, and so on until he feels he has recruited sufficient labor for the task at hand. He recruits just enough labor, for not only must he feed those working on his fields, but he knows that by asking them to help him, he has assumed an obligation to reciprocate. Occasionally, transplantation may be complete, leaving the original seed bed fallow; more usually it involves thinning out the original seeding field and replanting elsewhere what has been removed. Villagers explain the necessity for transplanting in terms of saving the plants culled from the broadcast field, and also by the fact that yields are increased by the transplantation. While the seedlings are usually arranged roughly in rows, there is no rule that they must be—as a matter of fact weeding (which is facilitated by row planting) is rarely undertaken. With the completion of transplantation, a cultivator is free to pay back his reciprocal obligations, or to work for wages on the fields of large landholders, as no attention is needed in his own fields until harvest any time from December through February. This relatively slack period is also the usual time of making repairs to houses and boats or seeking temporary employment elsewhere. In spite of the harvest ahead, the thoughts of most men now turn to the new fishing season just beyond.

Any time after the rice has matured and the rains have let up enough so that the cut grain has a good chance of not being soaked, harvesting may begin. As far as the rice goes, there is no urgency about this and it is normal for a man to think up reasons for postponing this unpleasant task. Except on very small holdings, harvesting also requires a group of helpers. With conscientious effort it takes a week to harvest a field and this is often stretched to two or three weeks. Each stalk of rice is individually cut against the harvester's palm with a special knife held in the same hand. It is this slow process coupled with the necessary bent posture which is responsible for the negative attitudes held by most villagers about rice harvesting. The harvested heads of rice are tied in convenient-sized bundles and stacked at the edge of the field to be taken back to the village in the evening. The harvested stalks are left standing in the fields and serve as convenient fodder for village cattle, thereby ensuring fertilization of the fields for the following year's crop.

Before storage of the rice, about 5 percent of the total yield is set aside for seed the following year. The rest is kept, unwinnowed, either in special granaries outside the house or in large covered baskets in the kitchen. During lulls in women's activities, portions of the stored rice will be winnowed and restored either in baskets or 5-gallon kerosene tins. Only small quantities of rice are milled at a time, as milled rice does not keep as well as unmilled. During the past ten years there has been a considerable change in rice-milling facilities. Traditionally, each woman would grind her own rice in a large wooden mortar and pestle arrangement; however, with the introduction into the area of gasoline-powered engines, commercial rice mills have almost entirely superseded hand grinding in all but the most remote inland villages. In 1954 most of the women of Rusembilan took their rice for milling to the mill at the junction of the village road with the main highway into Pattani. For political reasons this mill was closed, and the Imam of Rusembilan in 1959 began operating a small mill within the village itself. The Imam's mill was never popular with the village women because of its small size, as there was considerable wastage of the rice itself, and the rice flour valuable for medical purposes as well as chaff for chicken feed was entirely lost. A new, large mill has since opened along the Pattani highway, and while its distance from Rusembilan is an inconvenience, it is used almost exclusively by the village women.

Villagers estimate that it takes somewhat more than 2 acres of *padi* field to meet the rice consumption needs of a small-to-average family. Most families in Rusembilan own no more than an acre, so that rice deficit is widespread throughout the village and other villages like it. In an effort to improve this situation, and to provide grain for the northeastern provinces of Thailand, district authorities planted a large demonstration field of rice during the spring of 1964 (out of season) which depended on irrigation for flooding the fields. Each village in the district was assigned a particular 4-acre plot in the field and was responsible for transplanting, weeding (which was necessary at this season), and harvesting it. An unexpected problem arose: this was the only field of rice within many miles at this season and it consistently attracted a tremendous concentration of birds. The solution, only partially effective, was to draw up a roster from each village of men owning firearms and attempt to keep one on guard at all times. When the rice was ready for harvest, the rainy season had already set in and much of the grain which had escaped the depredations of birds was beaten from the stalks by the downpours. The outlook for more than one crop of rice each year is therefore not very bright, particularly as in the coastal villages very few of the men are willing to sacrifice time to rice which they could be using for fishing.

In general, the people of Rusembilan have little interest in raising vegetables and other garden crops for their own consumption. Some, however, do maintain small gardens which are carefully fenced to exclude freely wandering cattle. These gardeners are usually among the less wealthy residents of the village who cannot be sure of sufficient income from fishing to supply them with vegetables from the Pattani market. Perhaps two dozen Rusembilan families raise *ubi keladi,* a form of taro which is used as a supplemental source of starch in the diet. Sweet manioc (*ubi kayu*) is a popular root crop; however, the inconvenience of transplantation keeps many families from growing this crop. A few families plant patches of okra, melons, and pineapple on whatever plot of waste land they can find and fence. In addition to the garden crops, a number of individuals own fruit- or nut-producing trees. Mangos grown in the village are of no economic and little dietary importance, but they are a delight to small children who manage to consume most of the crop as it ripens. Bananas, papayas, and a caramelly, brown-skinned fruit called *sawahnillo* are grown by some families for domestic consumption, while cashew nuts are grown for sale by a few others.

Plantations in a Cash Economy

Second only to fish as economic resources of South Thailand are plantation crops. Regionally, rubber is by far the most important of these cash crops, but along the coast coconuts predominate. Coastal villagers, of course, are not unaware of their own hinterlands, so the possibility or actuality of growing rubber is not alien to the thoughts of these fishermen. Because of a marked downward trend in the availability of *kembong* in waters accessible to village fishermen, and to decrease in net income from fishing, a large number of men from Rusembilan and other fishing villages have seriously entertained the idea of taking up rubber production, at least on a part-time basis, to tide them over what they are confident is only a temporary slump in their fishing luck. Attention is directed toward rubber rather than coconuts because most of the land suitable for commercial coconut growing is already occupied, while vast tracts of land suitable for growing rubber are available in the sparsely populated interior.

The pattern of land utilization in Rusembilan is typical of these coastal villages. Approximately half of the village lands are controlled by nonresident owners for growing coconuts. These owners are mostly the Chinese merchants in the town of Pattani, and while they certainly make a profit *in absentia,* their plantations in the village do provide gainful employment for a number of village families who work as plantation guards and harvesters. Another 10 percent of village lands is used by residents of Rusembilan for commercial coconut production. The average size of locally owned plantations is about an acre and a half, compared with a little over 10 acres' average holding for nonresidents. Coconut production as a supplementary occupation is ideally suited to the seasonal round in Rusembilan as the nuts mature throughout the year and can be picked more or less casually when it is convenient for the owner (or caretaker). It is customary to harvest each tree at ninety-day intervals, during which time half a dozen nuts will have ripened. On small plantations of up to about one hundred trees, picking can be done informally by young boys who are always glad to shinny up the trees and throw down the ripe nuts. On larger holdings it is customary to hire a professional picker. There are now five such men in Rusembilan; each owns a specially trained monkey who is sent up into the tree with instructions as to which nuts to harvest.[2] An efficient monkey can pick 400 or 500 coconuts a day for which his owner receives payment at a rate of 8 *baht* (40 cents) per hundred. After the ripe nuts are harvested they are split and dried for a day. This has the effect of shrinking the meat of the nut so that it can be easily removed from the shell, after which it is dried for two more days before sale to dealers in Pattani as copra. Splitting and drying are ordinarily the work of women and children, although on large plantations men may lend a hand if the volume of nuts is great. Over the eight-year period, the price villagers obtained for copra just about doubled, so that a man with a plantation of one hundred trees could generally count on an annual income of from 6000 to 7000 *baht* ($300–$350).

While the proportion of Rusembilan men with proprietary interest in rubber plantations remained much the same between 1956 and 1964 (about 10 percent), the individuals involved have changed; in fact only two men who had acquired rubber-growing land in 1956 maintained their interest in it at all. The reason for this turnover is that rubber growing does not provide quick and easy profit. Most of the land acquired is uncleared jungle which must be prepared before planting the rubber trees. Working full time at clearing the jungle, a man can prepare at most 2 acres in a month. Full-time work is the exception rather than the rule, however, because commitments to rice and fishing at home usually limit time at the plantation to intermittent three- or four-day periods. Also, if clearing is not kept up conscientiously, the jungle quickly reclaims the land which had been cleared. Coupled with this is the problem of malaria—coastal villages are practically free of this disease and fishermen staying for any length of time in the malarial interior are likely to be striken with the disease. Most of the men from Rusembilan are ready to give up rubber growing at this point; a few con-

---

[2] These monkeys will ordinarily harvest ripe coconuts; however, if their handler specifies *"muda-muda"* (young or unripe) they will throw down green nuts.

tinue and plant trees. Until recently, the only available rubber saplings were of a variety which took seven years to mature to the point at which they would produce any rubber at all. During this period constant attention is required to keep unwanted growth down and all that can be gleaned from the plantation is dry rice and annual vegetable crops, providing for the cultivator no more than subsistence. In 1964 only one of the two men still involved after eight years in rubber growing was producing latex for sale.

There are indications that this involvement with rubber growing will change in the years to come. Probably most of the men of Rusembilan now committed to rubber growing will continue in this pursuit. While most of the men owning rubber lands in 1956 were at least moderately wealthy men with strong ties and numerous commitments to their home village, many of the present rubber proprietors are less well-to-do and have severed their relationships with Rusembilan. They do not maintain membership on *kolek* crews, nor do they have many kinsmen in the village. In addition, most of them have now sold their houses in Rusembilan and taken up permanent residence on their plantations. Economic conditions in the coastal villages are becoming worse rather than better. There are less fish available and there is more competition for positions on the "lucky" boats. Rice lands are becoming depleted through salinization. On the other hand, the Thai government is subsidizing the planting (and replanting) of new varieties of rubber which not only yield several times as much latex as the old type, but will mature within as few as four years. With the increase of hire-tapping as a secondary occupation, more and more coastal people are becoming acclimatized to the environment of the interior. The growth of new frontier settlements is rapidly removing isolation as a source of discontent to individual small holders.

One of the problems still facing the aspiring rubber producer is that of acquiring clear legal title to his plantation. Neither Malay villagers nor local Thai officials are quite sure of the technicalities involved. Formerly, most such land was acquired by outright purchase from the government or by paying up the defaulted taxes of a previous owner. Both of these methods required considerable red-tape and documentation in a language foreign to the villager. The most common method of acquiring land today is simply to squat on it. Although the only case of squatting in the area to be legally resolved was resolved to the detriment of the squatters—they were evicted after an investment of four years of effort, villagers are optimistic about the outcome of other squatting situations.

One group of ten families from Rusembilan in 1961 decided to try their hand as a group at plantation life. These families had been outside of the mainstream of village life in Rusembilan, both physically and socially. They lived in poorer than average houses at the western edge of the village. Few of them had close relatives in Rusembilan, and while most of the men did have positions on boat crews, these were on the cooperative *kolek* whose fishing success had never been spectacular. None of them owned *padi* fields or coconut land. With little to hold them, they were positively inclined to move when it was heard that there was unused land suitable for mixed rubber and fruit production in an area about 25 miles from Rusembilan. Within the district where they were to settle, the government had already established a resettlement project where Thai farmers, mostly from the distant central and northeastern parts of the country, were allotted 25 *rai* (about 10 acres) of land. If they maintained it properly for a period of five years it was to be granted with clear title to the settlers. The district officer who was approached by the families from Rusembilan apparently based his response to their inquiries on the pattern established for the resettlement project. Each of the ten families was allowed to use a parcel of 25 *rai* and was told by the district officer, "You do your planting and never mind about the future." They interpreted this as a promise that they would eventually be given title to the land. In addition to this, the district officer told them that further plots of 10 *rai* each would be made available to the families for rice planting, and that the district would supply the first year's seed. In addition to planting rubber, some of it of the early-maturing, high-yield variety, these families have also established a fair number of coconut and fruit trees, including durian, rambutan, and some citrus fruits. In order to produce sufficient income during the period required for the trees to mature, most of the men engage in fishing occupations either at Rusembilan or Pattani. Only two have retained boat crew membership at Rusembilan, but it is often possible for others to substitute for a regular crew member who is unable to fish on a particular night. The semicommercial fishing operations from Pattani, to be discussed in the following section, are the most attractive part-time fishing occupations available to these men. However, if the competition is too intense to enable them to be taken on either kind of fishing boat, they are willing to do whatever other kinds of odd laboring jobs they can find. In spite of the apparent economic insecurity, after three years these ten families still view their move as advantageous. They speak of the nearby village as a "good" village, with many congenial Malays; they point to a good school, and more important, excellent religious instruction for their children. And although they admit that, "now it is difficult to get money," all families agree that their new life is preferable to life at Rusembilan.

Hire-tapping is an occupation which is spreading rapidly among the people of Rusembilan and other coastal villages. Typically this is an occupation in which a married couple takes part as a team. Like the emerging pattern of squatting on rubber land, it is an occupation favored mostly by the less well-to-do members of the community, that is, families who do not own rice-growing land. In 1964 an estimated forty couples left Rusembilan at the close of the *kembong* season—actually many had left before the end of fishing—and proceeded inland to areas where they had friends and relatives. With these contacts it was possible to find a plantation owner who could use extra help in tapping his trees. These plantation owners belong neither to the category of true small holders, who are able to tap their own trees, nor to the large plantation owners (both Thai and Malay) who insist on a high degree of tapping skill on the part of their employees. They belong to a large middle range group whose technical standards in terms of planting, tapping, and processing are considerably below those that the government (and consumers of latex) would like to see. Under a hire-tapping arrangement, the tapping couple, equipped with miner's lamps, will begin collecting raw latex shortly after midnight, continuing work until about nine in the morning. After collection, the raw latex is strained to rid it of impurities—in this type of operation it is usually strained through moss and dried grass—and put to coagulate with the addition of a small amount of acetic acid in kerosene tins cut in half lengthwise. Within thirty minutes the latex has coagulated and can be put through two sets of presses, reminiscent of clothes wringers, emerging as large rubbery sheets, in which form it is sold to dealers for further processing and fabrication. In the course of their daily tapping a couple can collect about 15 kilograms of latex for which they are paid 50 percent of the sale price. Because of tremendous fluctuations in the price of rubber on the international market, this can bring a tapping couple anywhere from about 45 to 175 *baht* ($2.25–$8.75) or more a day, although recently their wages have been consistently closer to the lower figure. After the rainy season the couples return to Rusembilan, "when money in the village is easy," that is, when the prawn season has started.

In 1956, before the opportunities for hire-tapping had become so widespread, it was customary for a group of men from Rusembilan to travel to northwestern Malaya to augment the labor force of rice harvesters there. During the Malayan rice harvest, which occurred before that of the east coast Thai provinces, the Malayan government allowed temporary labor to come in from Thailand without passports. Although villagers from Rusembilan do not care for the job of rice harvesting, many took this opportunity to travel to Malaya on the chance they might find other, more palatable employment. With the increase in hire-tapping needs in South Thailand, however, and the relatively good rate of pay, individuals from Rusembilan no longer take advantage of the chance to seek employment in Malaya.

Economic Specialists and the Market Town

Most of the residents of Rusembilan and other coastal villages in South Thailand confine their activities largely to traditional pursuits—fishing and agriculture—within the village. However, a small but increasing number of individuals have become involved in economic dealings with ramifications far beyond their own village. The coastal villages as a whole are far better integrated into the cash-based market system, and far more dependent upon it than are the more nearly self-sufficient interior Malay communities of South Thailand. The obvious reason for this situation is that the village fishing industry on the coast could not exist without a demand for its products beyond the village. It is the women of these fishing villages who have led the way into the national cash economy through their almost daily dealings with wholesale fish dealers. Here they receive cash for their produce, which in turn they budget among the necessary and desirable items in the town market. Until fairly recently the men of Rusembilan had little or nothing to do with the economic side of Pattani life, their contacts being confined to periodic carnivals and to dealings (as infrequently as possible) with district authorities.

Within the village, however, a number of men, preferring for one reason or another not to fish, have acquired somewhat specialized economic roles. Chief among these is the coffee shop (*kedai kopi*) owner. The coffee shop owner requires first of all a "shop." This is nothing more than a very simply constructed shed with thatched roof and often only woven bamboo walls. Unlike houses, the coffee shop is erected directly on the ground, the natural sand serving as floor. Within this building are two or three rough board tables with equally rough benches on either side. All that is necessary beyond this is a supply of tea and sweetened condensed milk and some means of heating water. However, usually, a coffee shop will also sell a variety of inexpensive groceries and dry goods such as biscuits, cigarettes, pocket knives, detergent, kerosene, needles, a few nonperishable vegetables and occasionally coffee. There has been a tendency since 1960 for the variety of goods stocked to decrease. The number of coffee shops itself has decreased from five at that time to three in 1964. This situation has been brought about by the combination of less cash in the village and the absolute decrease in the amount of time spent in the coffee shops by village fishermen. This latter phenomenon will be discussed in the following chapter and again in Chapter 7.

The busiest time for the coffee shops is during the morning hours, after the *kolek* have returned from fishing. As the men hand over the distribution and selling of the fish to their wives, many wander off to the coffee shops to relax, talk, and to refresh themselves with hot tea (served with an almost equal amount of sweetened condensed milk.) Rarely does the customer buy more than one glass of tea, although he may remain sitting in the shop for well over an hour. Consequently, even when business is brisk, the owner is fortunate if he grosses 40 to 50 *baht* ($2.00–$2.50) a day on the sale of tea at 1 *baht* per glass. Perhaps an equal amount can be made selling other odds and ends to housewives who have forgotten to obtain the item at market. Cigarettes, once a significant item in coffee shop trade, are still stocked but rarely sold. Men feel that cash is too scarce to squander on commercial cigarettes when they can make their own with inexpensive local tobacco and nipa leaves (these items are provided free of charge at each coffee shop table). Ordinarily, a shop owner will have some other occupation to supplement his income. One owner in 1964 took on pupils for religious instruction, another owned a small coconut plantation, and the third dabbled in carpentry, politics, and filled in on several boat crews in case of temporary vacancies.

Other specialized occupational roles to be found in Rusembilan include most importantly those concerned with spiritual matters, ranging from the curing of illnesses on the one hand to educating the young on the other. These are the roles of *bomo* and Imam to be described in Chapters 5 and 6. There are several other services which are performed within the village of Rusembilan. The need for them is sporadic rather than continuing and they are not really essential to the village economy. Among these, the making of *belachan,* or shrimp paste, has already been mentioned. A number of men engage in rigging the various types of nets used in village fishing operations. This involves attaching lead sinkers to the bottom of the nets, and fashioning and attaching wooden floats to the top. The need for this type of activity has declined since the introduction of nylon nets with a much longer life expectancy than cotton. A number of men and women in Rusembilan have tried their hand at shirt and blouse tailoring respectively, although in 1964 there was none. (Tailoring can be done very quickly and inexpensively in the Pattani market where the cloth itself is sold.) In 1960 a coconut plantation owner in Rusembilan, in order to utilize more fully his resources, began weaving hats out of fallen coconut palm fronds. He found that there was absolutely no market for these hats in Rusembilan and that the town market price for them was too low to make it worth his while to continue his sideline occupation.

There are a number of specialized occupations involved in house construction. Although all men of Rusembilan are capable carpenters, a small number are highly skilled in woodworking. These men, who generally learned their skills from their fathers, are able with amazing accuracy and speed to rough out mortise and tenon joints, to shape the wooden pegs for securing the joints, and to produce a number of fine articles of furniture. They are in great demand whenever a house is to be built, being called in wherever precise workmanship is crucial. Traditionally, these services were paid for by the return of other services on the part of the house owner, but increasingly today reciprocation is being replaced by cash payment. One skilled carpenter in Rusembilan constructed his own *kolek*, a tedious and painstaking task to say the least. While several other men in the village are able to, and occasionally do, construct the smaller and cruder types of boats for themselves, all, except this one man, purchase their *kolek* from the village of Taluban, 30 miles down the coast, where boat building of the highest order is a village specialization. (Boats from Taluban are sold up and down the east coast as far north as Nakorn Sritamarat and as far south as Trengganu in Malaysia.) Other minor occupations related to house building such as casting of the concrete blocks used as footings for house posts, manufacture of the decorative wooden scrollwork placed at the top of the window opening in more substantial village houses, and the preparation of roofing thatch from coconut or nipa palm fronds for less substantial village houses are carried on as the need arises—or if not, can be provided by craftsmen in Pattani.

Pattani town is becoming increasingly important to the Malay villages of South Thailand as an economic focus. The coastal villages are less able to maintain any semblance of isolated self-sufficiency. At present, the Pattani municipal market is the center of this focus, although an additional market center is being planned for the town. Within the large covered structure, both Thai and Malay women squat with their goods for sale. The bulk of the goods sold within the market is foodstuffs: staples such as rice, a variety of dried beans and peas, fresh vegetables and fruits, eggs and seasonings. Interspersed among these are to be found assorted items of hardware. Beyond this largest section of the market is sold an assortment of brightly colored sweet cakes and candies, and beyond that is the section devoted to dry goods. Here is a wide array of sarongs, inexpensive printed ones from Japan or Thailand, plaids for men woven in India, and expensive beautifully hand-stamped batiks from Indonesia. Also found in this section are the brightly colored yard goods used to make up blouses and the dresses increasingly being worn by young Malay girls as well as townspeople. Here also are located the seamstresses seated at their treadle sewing machines ready to sew up a sarong (the word *sarong* means "sheath" or "tube") on the spot or fashion a blouse or dress while the customer browses further through the market. Meat and a small amount of fish are sold in a special wing of the market. This wing was built in 1960 with gleaming elevated counter spaces and full screening against ever-present flies. By 1964 the meat wing was as dirty and foul-smelling as any in southern Thai towns, its screens deteriorated or torn out long since. Around this nucleus some village women vend their fish, preferring the occasional jostling for position to paying municipal rent for a reserved seat at (more correctly, *on*) the counter. Fish sales are usually confined to the morning hours, their place being taken in the afternoon by women bearing baskets of plantation products: durian, rambutan, and *petai,* long beanlike pods harvested from jungle trees. The whole market place is girded by a roadway which is clogged by pedestrian and motor traffic. While the Pattani bus terminal is located two blocks from the market, all but the large intercity busses carry passengers bound directly for the market. Obligingly they bypass the terminal to take their human and vegetal cargo to their place of business, wait for them, and return thence to their villages. Built on medium-duty truck chassis, the busses when divested of the bundles, bicycles, and vegetables on top and a number of clinging passengers on the sides, look rather like enlarged, aluminum station wagons.

Across this roadway from the market are the establishments of merchants and dealers, largely Chinese but including also some Malays and Indians. Many of these shops attempt to stock as wide a supply of goods as is possible, like little department stores. Others deal in a single line such as dry goods (mainly in the hands of Indians) or groceries. It is here that the fish dealers have their collection points for village fish—usually their packing and distribution centers are elsewhere. Along the streets making up the rest of Pattani are situated similar shops, branches of four Bangkok banks, a number of hotels and restaurants, and small manufacturing and repair facilities of one sort or another. There are also several large importing firms in various parts of the town, mostly inconspicuous to the unaccustomed eye, but including one which has recently moved into a large new building with a full-fronted display window behind which can be seen brand-new Fords and Toyotas, and an assortment of tractors and farm machinery. It is mainly these large importers, along with the fish wholesalers and bankers (when, in fact, these three roles are not combined in one person) who comprise the economic elite of Pattani.

Because of the frequency of such multiple roles, the villager from Rusembilan is apt to find himself in a set of multiple relationships with the same businessman. While this situation is potentially exploitable by the businessman, and indeed is often exploited in other parts of Southeast Asia, Pattani businesses are by and large extremely honest in their dealings with villagers. With the rush to motorize *kolek,* especially between 1958 and 1959, a large number of Malay villagers were forced to go into debt to the town merchants. There was no general pattern to the arrangement of these loans, although most were treated as installment buying. In most cases the villager was made to feel that he was getting a "good deal." This was accomplished either by not charging the highest legal interest rate of 15 percent, by allowing a certain amount of time before interest would be charged on the outstanding amount, or by imposing no penalties if the purchaser was unable to meet one (or sometimes more) installment. On the other hand, some form of hidden interest was usually collected by the merchant, such as imposing a contract on the villager to supply all his shares of fish to the merchant at a price slightly below the going rate, or obligating him to make all of his gasoline purchases from the merchant at a price somewhat higher than usual. In general, however, relations between the merchants and the Malay villagers have been extremely good: each is happy with his end of the installment arrangements. The merchant, wary of the political situation in South Thailand, is careful not to offend the Malay, who in turn finds the merchant (almost always Chinese) to be more sympathetic and usually honest than the Thais with whom he comes in contact.

One example of the developing relationships between Chinese merchants and Malay villagers is the middle-scale fishing operations referred to earlier in this chapter. In 1958, at the time that nylon nets became the rule in this area, an enterprising fisherman and respected steerer conceived the notion of seeking capital to finance fishing operations with larger boats and further offshore than was possible with *kolek* and traditional fishing methods. The result was that this individual entered into an equal partnership with the son of the largest fish wholesaler in Pattani. Through this arrangement they had acquired by 1964 two 60-foot motor launches with refrigeration facilities. Each boat carries a crew of four in addition to the captain; crew members are recruited on the basis of strength and ability and may come from as far away as Songkhla. As in traditional methods, operations are confined to the dark of the moon; however, the contract period is limited to a single lunar period, a new crew being taken on at the next dark moon. The boats go to sea and remain for anywhere from three to seven days, often fishing for large (and valuable) species of fish 100 or more miles off shore. At the end of each lunar period accounts are settled. First, costs of fuel, ice, food, and net depreciation are subtracted. Of the remaining proceeds, the owners receive four shares, the captain receives two shares, and each crew member receives one share (a total of ten shares). A typical month's gross on these operations may be as high as 20,000 *baht* ($1000), which even after subtraction of operating costs provides each crewman with quite a good income.

The fish caught in this deep-sea operation are handled differently from the traditional village catches. The larger species are in great demand in the Malaysian cities to the south and to a lesser extent in Bangkok. All of the fish dealers in Pattani keep in touch daily with the market prices in Penang—usually by means of the evening report on Radio Malaysia, but often by special telegraphic contact. When these species are available locally the dealers transport them daily by truck to Penang, some six hours by road, and twice a week by rail to Bangkok. As there are no market reports on the Thai radio, dealers must rely entirely on telegraphic reporting of Bangkok prices. This, coupled with the more difficult packing and longer transport, makes them favor the Malaysian market over the Bangkok market unless there is a significant difference in price.

The increasing complexity of fishing operations in South Thailand, starting with motorized tow boats, the motorization of individual *kolek,* middle-scale operations as described above, and involvement with an international market represents a trend which in all probability will continue. Already large-scale Thai-Chinese fishing operations are being carried out in the offshore waters of the Gulf of Thailand and the South China Sea. Japanese fishermen are experimenting with new and more efficient netting techniques, and international oceanographic teams have established that the marine resources in these waters are perhaps the most abundant in the world—and are only waiting to be more efficiently exploited as one of the solutions to the problems of Southeast Asia. More will be said of this trend in the final chapter, and of the tremendous implications it holds for the economy and total way of life of Rusembilan and other peasant fishing villages both in South Thailand and in peninsular Malaysia.

3

The Web of Life

The Family and Household

THE BASIC SOCIAL and economic unit in the coastal Malay villages is the nuclear family. At times the nuclear family is subordinated to other groups for special activities such as *kembong* fishing and rice transplantation and harvesting, but these larger units are at best temporary and unstable. The nuclear family persists as that group in which the fundamental division of labor of the society is reflected, and which for most purposes can function as an independent unit. The nuclear family, as indeed all kin relationships, is structured bilaterally—no more weight being given to one side than to the other. It emphasizes within it the relationships of husband-wife, parent-child, and sibling-sibling, differing in these respects from our own family system only in that the sibling-sibling relationship tends to remain stronger after the grown children have married and moved out to establish their own nuclear family units.

Within the family it is the husband who is the main provider, engaging in the major occupations of fishing, rice cultivation, and plantation management. He is nominally head of the family and dispenser of authority, although his absence from the house usually results in the delegation of this role to his wife or to an elder child or children. It is also the husband who represents the family in the religious and political activities of the community. While women may take secondary roles in religious matters often only as observers, they play no part at all in the area of political decision making. The wife's role is that of manager of the household. She, with the aid of her elder daughters, takes care of domestic chores such as keeping the house clean, maintaining a supply of wood for cooking and water for drinking and washing (bathing is not performed in the house but at one of the several wells located throughout all Malay villages), taking care of infants, who after they are weaned are passed into the care of elder siblings, and preparing food for the whole family. As indicated in the last chapter, an important role played by wives in fishing villages is that of distribution and marketing of fish. Children are expected to be respectful toward and to obey both their parents and their elder siblings. From earliest childhood, however, they are treated by other members of the family as individuals with their own rights and obligations: authority over them is never exercised indiscriminately by their elders. As children grow they are expected to assume a greater share of the daily routine appropriate to their sex. It is common to see a six-year-old girl (or boy, for infant care is not restricted to females) playing on the beach in complete charge of her infant sibling. One of the first responsibilities given to young boys is tending cattle. The boy may take up to a dozen head of cattle out to pasture in the morning, guard them, and return to the village with them in the early or middle afternoon. As a girl approaches puberty she spends more and more time with her mother and any other mature female members of the family practicing the domestic arts she will need for married life, and by the time she has become a young woman she will never be seen walking or playing in the village, being in virtual seclusion until marriage. Ordinarily, boys of the same age will begin a period of apprentice fishing, going along with their father's fishing crew as an extra member who, nonetheless, is entitled to his full share of the catch.

The following account, quoted from the original study of Rusembilan (Fraser 1960: 128–131) illustrates the typical make-up of a well-respected prosperous family in Rusembilan:

The house is elevated about ten feet on stilts, and this provides a work and storage place below as well as protection from monsoon floods. The house itself is built of wood with a clay tile roof. It has a large living, dining, and sleeping room with a smaller sleeping room at either of the back corners of the main room. The floor is built on four levels with a difference of about eight inches between each. . . . The corridor between the two smaller rooms serves as a pantry for the kitchen, which is erected against the back wall of the house proper. Over the doors and windows in the main room are ornate Islamic designs similar to those used on the *kolek,* and hanging on the wall are photographs of the family, quotations from the Koran, and pictures of Mecca. This room also contains two tables, a storage cabinet, two mirrors, a wall clock, and twelve to fifteen woven grass mats for sleeping and sitting.

The head of the household, called *Pak Sa (pak besar,* big father) by all the villagers, is sixty, and his wife *Mak Sa* is fifty. In theory, they have authority over all members of the house, but rarely try to exercise it. With them live one son, thirty, who is attending a religious school [see Chapter 6] in the area and who comes home only for special occasions; a son, thirteen; and a daughter, eight. The couple has, living in the village, one married son and one married daughter whose children are often found in and around the grandparents' house, where they are sure to find greater indulgence and fewer chores. Another son, just recently married, was at the time of this study [1956] spending some time at the home of his wife and some time occupying one of the smaller chambers in his parents' house before settling permanently in a house of his own. *Pak Sa* says that he expects married children, before settling permanently, to live with one set of parents or the other in order to save money. His daughter and her husband lived with him for several months, and his son lived with his wife's parents. . . .

Pak Sa supports his family by growing rice and by fishing. He owns ten plots of padi field, three of which have been spoiled by salt-water flooding, and the rice that he plants on the remaining seven is sufficient for his family. He owns two head of cattle for plowing, a *kolek* of which he is steerer, and a *jokung* [a small one- or two-man boat]. He sums up his position by saying that he has many things but no money and does not consider himself particularly important in the community. Actually, although he holds no formal position in the village, *Pak Sa* is one of the respected individuals [*orang baik,* see Chapter 4] whose advice is frequently sought by people having difficulties. He believes that probably he will never make the pilgrimage to Mecca as he never has enough money. He is spending fifteen hundred baht ($75) yearly to support his son in religious school and has no surplus when the rice harvest and the fishing are poor. When his catch and harvest are good, he has no inclination to go to Mecca.[1]

By 1964, *Pak Sa* had retired from active fishing, although he still owned his own *kolek*. The son who was married and living in Rusembilan in 1956 had at that time been one of the most successful steerers on the beach. By 1964 he had acquired his own *kolek;* however, he no longer acted as steerer. What time he did devote to fishing was simply as a member of the crew of his own boat. More and more of his time was being invested in a small coconut plantation which he had acquired in a neighboring village, as well as in rice fields inherited from his father. The married daughter died in childbirth in 1960, leaving an eight-year-old son. Her husband, not a native of Rusembilan, remarried a woman from outside the village. For a year they continued living in Rusembilan, but because neither had any strong ties with the village, decided to take up plantation life as one of the ten families discussed in the last chapter. The husband is one of those men who does occasionally fish with the *kolek* of Rusembilan. His son is often to be found for relatively long periods of time with his grandfather, *Pak Sa.*

The son who married in 1956 died shortly thereafter, leaving no children. His wife returned to her own village and has since married a man with no connections in Rusembilan. Hussain, the religious student, completed his instruction and was financed by his father on a pilgrimage to Mecca. Returning in his new status of haji, he was able to marry into a very wealthy and influential inland family. He is now living with his father-in-law, also a haji, who owns a well-managed and productive rubber and fruit plantation of over 200 acres. However, he pays frequent visits to his parents and siblings in Rusembilan. The remaining son, twenty years old in 1964, was not yet married. Although *Pak Sa* had offered him a religious education and a trip to Mecca, he had chosen to follow a more traditional life in Rusembilan. He is well established on the crew of a successful *kolek* and is considered a leader with considerable potential by both

[1] © 1960 by Cornell University. Used by permission of Cornell University Press.

his peers and elder men of the village. *Pak Sa's* youngest daughter, only eight in 1956, is now married with two small children and with her husband is living permanently with *Pak Sa* and *Mak Sa*. Her husband has, like *Pak Sa's* youngest son, decided on a life of a village fisherman, and is also established with a successful boat crew.

The foregoing example of a typical high-status family in Rusembilan and its developments over the course of eight years illustrates a number of points concerning the social organization of coastal Malay villages. With few exceptions, marriage in these communities is exogamous, the bride and groom belonging to different villages. Marriage arrangements are *always* made by the parents of the prospective couple, and are usually initiated by the boy's father. During the time that a boy is approaching marriageable age, his father remains alert to potential mates in other villages throughout the region. Through his network of kin and ceremonial connections he is able to keep fair track of girls in a large number of villages, and to roughly assess their suitability for marriage with his son. The main criteria for choosing a daughter-in-law are beauty, family background, wealth, and religious training. These criteria are weighted equally, and any acceptable mate for one's son must possess at least one. *Pak Sa's* son Hussain because of his own background, relative wealth, and superior religious training, was able to obtain a wife who ranked high on all four of these criteria. Fathers seeking daughters-in-law, naturally, must balance objectively the assets of their sons against the assets they are seeking in his mate. When the field has been narrowed to one or a few suitable girls, the boy's father seeks the assistance of an intermediary, a man who is known to both families. It is this man who either arranges for a surreptitious viewing of the girl by the boy and his father, or enters directly into negotiations with her family. When the negotiations have been completed, the girl is informed by her parents of her impending marriage, and must begin making preparations for the wedding. The wedding ceremony itself, as part of the religious round of Rusembilan, will be discussed in Chapter 5.

Where a couple takes up residence after marriage is determined primarily by economic considerations. However, it is always preferable to live near one set of parents. Villagers in Rusembilan assert that there is a tendency for boys who have grown up in the village to settle in Rusembilan more frequently than in their bride's village. Their reason is that by the time of their marriage, boys will have become full-time fishermen, loath to give up their occupation for interior cultivation or even to make the readjustment to different fishing groups in other coastal villages. Statistics collected on marriages between 1956 and 1964 tend to bear this out, with nearly twice as many Rusembilan boys remaining in the village with their wives as moved to the village of their parents-in-law. With girls native to Rusembilan, on the other hand, almost exactly the same number moved to their husband's village as settled in Rusembilan. Away from the coast the tendency to virilocality (settling in the village of the groom) is somewhat stronger. On the coast this is offset to some extent by the fact that if a man from an inland area who has few land resources marries into Rusembilan he has a considerably better chance of making a fair living, without real assets, in fishing. Actually, the decision as to ultimate postmarital residence is usually not made immediately after marriage. A couple will ordinarily spend a period of up to a month first with one set of parents and then with the next, sometimes continuing this pattern for a year or two, before weighing all factors and finally deciding on a permanent home.

Another practice prevalent in the whole area keeps the tendency toward virilocality from becoming more universal. This is the case, as in *Pak Sa's* family, in which the youngest daughter tends to settle permanently with her parents, usually in the same household. There are advantages to this system for both the young couple and for the parents. The parents can count on being supported and taken care of in their old age, while the newly married couple has the advantage of stepping into a well-established domestic and often economic concern. At first the new couple is definitely a subordinate unit in the household, but over time the roles gradually change, and it is the daughter and her husband who are heads of the household, and her parents who are in a dependent position. On occasion, it will be the youngest son and his wife who take over as household heads, but it is felt by the old people of the village that it is preferable to retire from active life in the household of a daughter rather than a daughter-in-law. Although there is no hard-and-fast rule, the traditional system of inheritance tends to be employed and serves to even out potential inequalities arising from a situation of ultimogeniture. Under this sytem, the parents will begin distributing their property to sons and daughters when or shortly after the latter are married. It is often the case that the eldest, particularly if he is a male, will receive a slightly larger or a slightly better share than his younger siblings, but this is by no means always so. In *Pak Sa's* family, the eldest son certainly received more in the way of rice lands than other members of the family. However, the second son who received no real property considers that he has been fairly treated because his father used a large sum of money to finance his religious studies and his pilgrimage to Mecca. Of his two children remaining at home, his daughter and her husband will inherit *Pak Sa's* house and some of his remaining lands, while his son will fall heir, presumably shortly after his marriage, to the rest of the family land and to *Pak Sa's kolek*. While this system of inheritance is not strictly in accord with Islamic law, only in the event of a man dying intestate with property undistributed or if there is a controversy among the heirs concerning the distribution of property is the matter considered in the light of scriptural law.

Before considering the wider ramifications of kinship, there remains to be mentioned one relationship partly within the nuclear family and partly outside of it. This is the relationship between siblings. Unlike our own kinship system, the matter of sex of the related siblings is of somewhat less importance in Malay society than is relative age. This difference of emphasis is reflected in the terminology used both in referring to and addressing one's siblings: one's elder sister is *kakak,* and she is differentiated from elder brother, *abang;* however, with regard to one's younger siblings there is no differentiation according to sex, both are referred to and addressed as *adek.* (See Table 3 for a full presentation of kinship terms.) The terminological pattern is reflected in the behavior of sib-

TABLE 3

RUSEMBILAN KINSHIP TERMINOLOGY

Relationship (Generation)	Specific Term (reference)		General Term (address)	
	Male	Female	Male	Female
Grandparental				
Lineals	Tok	Tok	Tok	Tok
Collaterals	Tok	Tok	Tok	Tok
Parental				
Lineals	Bapa, pak	Mak	Pak	Mak
Collaterals				
older	Pak-lung	Mak-lung	Pachu	Machu
middle	Pak-ngah	Mak-ngah	Pachu	Machu
younger	Pak-su	Mak-su	Pachu	Machu
Own				
Lineals				
older	Abang	Kakak	Abang	Kakak
younger	Adek	Adek	Adek	Adek
Collaterals				
older	Sapupu	Sapupu	Abang	Kakak
younger	Sapupu	Sapupu	Adek	Adek
Children's				
Lineals	Awang, anak	Me, anak	Awang, anak	Me, anak
Collaterals	Anak-saudara	Anak-saudara	Awang, anak	Me, anak
Grandchildren's				
Lineals	Awang, anak	Me, anak	Awang, anak	Me, anak
Collaterals	Awang, anak	Me, anak	Awang, anak	Me, anak

lings, both as children within the household, and later as adults. One of the roles of elder children in a family, as already mentioned, is that of taking care of younger siblings, and a small child looks to his older brothers and sisters in much the same light as he does his father and mother. They are owed respect, and from them he can expect the exercise of authority and discipline. From the point of view of these elder siblings, their charges, whether male or female, are little differentiated: they are to be cared for, and kept from harm and from committing serious breeches in the standards of behavior appropriate to their age. In later life this same type of relationship persists, younger siblings seeking advice, support, and assistance from their elder brothers and sisters in case of trouble. This is often particularly true in the case of the youngest daughter. In this case the elder siblings in the family, already in a parentlike relationship with her, in addition find her at the focal point of family sentiments, their original household. Insofar as there is motivation to maintain family ties, and there usually is, this is expressed in terms of frequent contacts with the locus of the original family in the form of support and advice to its youngest female member, resident there.

The *Kampong:* Neighbors and Kinsmen

Although the nuclear family is the basic unit of society, the most important unit is often the village, or *kampong.* This is the social and territorial context in which most of an individual's daily and seasonal activities take place. From within the village all of the groups demanded by suprafamily cooperation are drawn, and it is here that one's most important kinsmen outside of the immediate family are most often to be found. Ordinarily there is little difficulty in defining a *kampong* or a village: it is a discrete settlement separated from other such settlements by agricultural or other uninhabited land. Occasionally difficulties are presented by the hiving off of satellite settlements, close but separated from the parent community and having intimate economic, social, and religious ties with it. This is the situation in Rusembilan where Kampong Rusembilan is clearly separable into three subunits: Kampong Pata, the "beach village," which is the center of economic and social activities; Kampong Surau, the "mosque village," inland some half a mile, where at least the formal religious activities of the total community are centered; and Kampong Baru, a "new village," recently settled further inland among the community's rice fields, which looks for all of its support either to the beach or to the mosque settlement. Because of the close interrelationships and dependencies among these three settlements, and because all are serviced by and within earshot of the single mosque and its drum, the residents of Rusembilan in most contexts consider the whole to comprise the *kampong.* Certainly in dealing with the outside it is one. More will be said about the *kampong* in its political and religious functions in the two following chapters. For the present, it will be considered as a clearly defined territorial unit within which various types of social grouping take place.

Table 3 indicates the terminology employed in addressing and referring to relatives in coastal villages such as Rusembilan. Attention has already been drawn to the fact that in the terms employed for siblings, relative age is an important consideration. It is apparent that this principle also applies to one's parents' generation. Even here, however, this distinction is generally not used in address, but only in referring to "uncles" and "aunts" in terms of their age status relative to one's parents. In the generations below the speaker, little distinction as to the type of relative is made: in reference one distinguishes between one's own children, "son," "daughter," or simply "child" and "child of a relative," but this distinction is not carried through to address, nor does it apply in generations further removed. Thus the only precise kinship distinctions tend to occur within the nuclear family unit. But even these are extended in common use. In fact, even when no relationship between two individuals exists, appropriate kin terms tend to be used. This has already been seen in the almost universal practice in Rusembilan of referring to and addressing the couple described in the preceding section as *Pak Sa* and *Mak Sa*. A few individuals on their own generation level, however will call them *abang, kakak,* or *adek*. Without the special position of respect of such men as *Pak Sa*, an elder villager is usually addressed as *pachu*; if he is very old, or highly respected he may even be addressed as *tok,* as in the case of *"tok Imam."*

Within the community it is difficult to generalize about the function of kinship beyond the nuclear family. On the one hand, because of the traditionally close relations already referred to between adult siblings, there is a tendency for their entire households to partake in these; a tendency for the relationships to be closer and contacts more frequent between cousins than between nonrelatives. On the other hand, it is not uncommon in Rusembilan for the very closeness of the sibling bonds to result in bitter conflict (usually over the distribution of land). In such cases, although kinship has provided the channel, the relationship is wholly negative. Only on two types of occasion is kinship employed as a specific means of organizing group activity. As already indicated, one of these is the labor force required during the rice growing cycle, at transplantation and harvest. Here, even though the work force is essentially a group of kinsmen, careful account is kept of time put in by each member so that strict reciprocation will be possible. Naturally, when conflict has disrupted close kin ties, these cannot be exploited for reciprocal agricultural labor. It is not uncommon, therefore, to find neighbors and fellow crew members, as well as kinsmen, involved in these activities.

Ceremonial observances of transition points in the life cycle (life crises) call for kin-group activity. Such events as birth, naming, puberty, pilgrimage, marriage, and death are celebrated as part of the religious calendar, and will be discussed in Chapter 5, but they are also important in bringing together and formally involving a larger group of kinsmen than ordinarily functions. This kind of kin grouping differs from that involved in the agricultural round in that exact reciprocation is not expected, although there is the obligation on the part of all to participate in the crisis rites of any relatives. The number of ceremonial roles involved in these rites is small. By far the largest area for kin participation is in the provision and preparation of food for the attendant feast. For large occasions this may entail extremely large amounts of rice, several sheep or even beef cattle, and two or three days spent in preparing cooking places and concocting the many cauldrons of rice and curry. Some means of sharing the expense and labor for these feasts is essential, and kinship, related as it is to the life cycle, provides the most convenient one.

Although there is no strong inclination on the part of coastal Malay villagers to enter into cooperative relationships with others, at times this is necessary. In Rusembilan the most persistent demand for cooperation is in fishing for *kembong* and for large prawns where both the equipment and the effort of a number of men is required. The formation of the boat crews toward this end was discussed in the last chapter: this is an area in which kinship plays little or no part. Although the boat crew is considered by villagers to be purely an *ad hoc* organization, it not only tends to be recognizable from season to season, but also to form at least the basis of a number of other groupings throughout the year. House building is an activity requiring a large labor force for a short period of time. The typical house in Rusembilan is prefabricated in that the framework of the walls and roof are constructed on the ground and erected when complete. The group called in to assist in this house raising is unlike the group called upon for agricultural assistance, for it is composed in large part of fellow crew members of the builder; and if more assistance than they can provide is required, a man will call on his close friends and neighbors (who may also be kinsmen) rather than specifically expoiting kinship channels. The work of erecting the house is under the authority of the master carpenter who is usually not the householder himself, and is usually completed within a morning—at any rate no longer than a day. Each member of the group enjoys a feast, part of which has been offered to the spirits of the house during a small ceremony in which strips of cloth are tied to a house post to please the spirits. In addition, each helper is entitled to reciprocation of services by the builder. Often, a builder will also ask assistance of the same group or a part of it in the tedious job of tiling the roof or thatching it with *atap* (palm leaf thatch). Similar groups function in the erection of public buildings and for other community projects under the leadership of the village headman (*kamnan*) or Imam. While every able-bodied male is expected to contribute to such projects, it is rare that all will work at once. When an individual does work it is usually with this same congenial group of men, largely members of the same *kolek* crew.

Boat crew relationships may also provide the basis for cooperative economic ventures such as purchasing plantation land. Here usually the cooperation is limited to pooling capital and support during the process of acquisition, the work on the plantation (and presumably the proceeds) being individual. Mention has already been made of the cooperatively owned *kolek,* which by definition involve the crew members as a proprietary group. Likewise, purchase of outboard motors for the *kolek* and, previously, of tow boats have logically utilized the existing structure of the boat crew as the cooperating organization.

Perhaps the most striking evidence of the cohesiveness and stability of the groups formed by members of the same crew is the clusters of men who once regularly frequented the coffee shops along the beach. Both in the past and at present it is customary for the older or more respected men of the community to spend a certain amount of time each morning sitting in one or another of the coffee shops and discussing various matters of interest with anyone wishing to drop in. The amount of time thus spent by these men is determined in part by the press of other activities on the beach or in the fields; in part it is also determined by the continuity and size of their "audiences." Younger men drop in for a half and hour or more, and in this way much of the business of the village, and its important decisions are accomplished. In 1956, largely because of a greater abundance of money in Rusembilan, this practice of dropping in to have a glass of tea and to listen to the elders was more prevalent than it was in 1964. By and large at that time the group frequenting any one coffee shop tended to parallel closely the boat crew organization. The focal point of these groups, the elder, was usually either a boat owner or steerer, or both; his audience was usually composed of members of his own boat crew. Because *kolek* returned to the beach at different times during the early morning, the crew of any one *kolek* provided the only reliable group context for this activity. It was rare to find a total crew within a coffee shop at a given time: many men went directly to their houses for sleep, others drifted in later after performing other chores. Usually also one coffee shop would be the focal point of more than one *kolek* crew; and this had a tendency to create closer bonds between members of these crews than with others. These bonds played an important part in the development of the tow groups discussed in Chapter 7.

By 1964, attendance by common crew members at the coffee shops on anything like a regular basis had ceased almost completely. Many of the elders, in fact, no longer made a practice of regular attendance. Instead, many of the respected steerers and boat owners would sit on the beach, or a raised bamboo platform, in the shade of a coconut tree and serve as much the same kind of focal point as they had previously in the coffee shops. The clientele of the coffee shops themselves seems to have undergone a transformation: no longer do they reflect the organization of fishing as the dominant economic activity, but rather they seem to have become foci of special interest groups. In one of the Rusembilan coffee shops, the topic discussed almost to the exclusion of any other is Islam. This shop is owned by the father-in-law of the Imam, a haji himself, and its customers are mostly those people in the community who are influential or at least interested in religious affairs. A casual customer will drop into this shop if he has a particular religious question on which he wants advice (or if he has specific business of a secular nature with the owner or one of the regular customers). Further along the beach is a coffee shop in which the chief topic of conversation is political. This ranges from matters of village leadership and authority, through relations with district and provincial government officials, to questions involving the Thai nation and relations with peninsular Malaysia. The difference in the special interests represented by these two shops was illustrated during the summer of 1964 prior to the visit by the Queen Mother of Thailand to Pattani. A two-part order had been issued by the district office requesting each village in the district to decorate its "most beautiful" boat and form a part of the flotilla to greet the Queen Mother as she left her ship from Bangkok off Pattani and proceeded to the town by barge. The second part of the order required that the religious leadership of each village contribute to a fund to clean the new Pattani mosque (see Chapter 4) and be on hand when the Queen Mother came to inspect it. It is not surprising that the Queen Mother's visit as a general political move, as well as the advisability and details of Rusembilan's participation in the flotilla were constant topics of conversation at the politically oriented coffee shop, nor that the order having to do with the mosque was discussed at the religiously oriented shop. What was striking in this situation was that the topics were discussed at the respective shops to the *exclusion* of each other. The Imam of Rusembilan, who naturally was involved in participation during the visit in the mosque, was also interested in preparing a boat for the flotilla. However, when he wished to discuss the latter topic, he would remove himself to the coffee shop in which it was appropriate. The remaining coffee shop in Rusembilan in 1964, situated between the other two along the beach, retained the largest amount of the earlier flavor. Quite frequently *Pak Sa* and one or two other retired or retiring boat owners and steerers would congregate in this shop to talk about whatever matters were of interest (usually fishing) and off and on they would be joined by younger fishermen of the community— although no longer on the basis of boat crew affiliation—as in the past.

The Region: Kin and Ceremonial Networks

Outside of the *kampong* is an extensive area in South Thailand and northern Malaya in which the villager from Rusembilan finds he must operate on a number of occasions. The most universal dealing an individual has with other communities is in relation to marriage. Because of village exogamy, spouses must be chosen from an alien village, and the bulk of the relatives of at least one of the partners reside somewhere else. The intervillage relationships established through marriage or a series of marriages serve as basic channels which can be exploited for other purposes requiring intervillage contact. The most important usage of these relationships is participation in feasts; and this participation, in turn, periodically reinforces and validates the relationships for other forms of exploitation.

These feasts, usually simply called *makan pulot*, "eating (glutenous) rice," form a necessary part of all important religious ceremonies, as well as those marking transitions in an individual's life cycle. In addition, especially during the months immediately following Ramadan, the fasting month, large numbers of *makan pulot* are held throughout the area for no specific ceremonial purpose, but rather as pleasant and prestige-enhancing social events. The larger a *makan pulot*, the better. Invitations are sent out some time before the feast to all one's friends and relatives in the community, and to all friends, relatives, and affinal connections in other villages. Usually, if it is to be a successful feast, each of those invited is encouraged to bring along some of his friends or connections, so that often a man from Rusembilan, for instance, will receive an invitation from a man he knows in another village requesting him to attend a feast in a third village being given by a man he does not know. Acceptance of such invitations establishes a relationship between the two hitherto unknown individuals and refusal without extremely important reasons is an affront to the intermediary. Specifically, this relationship requires reciprocation at some later date by the man invited, while, most important, a new contact has been established which is potentially useful in a variety of contexts.

Preparations for large feasts involve considerable expenditure and effort, cooks and servers being kept busy throughout the day (or more) of feasting as new installments of guests are seated in small circles on the floor as soon as the previous group has finished. Feasts lasting two days are not uncommon, some have even gone on for three, during which time three to four thousand guests can be fed. The outlay of money for all this, however, is not lost, for each guest is expected to pay for his meal. Close friends, relatives, and neighbors contribute 10 *baht* (50 cents) or more, while ordinarily guests from other villages will contribute only half that. In the past it was common for a man to make a profit by giving a feast; today, although it is still possible to do so through extremely good management, it is more common to suffer a slight financial loss. However, the attendant gain in prestige for giving a large and generous feast is worth the price. When *makan pulot* are held in connection with religious or life crisis rites, it is obvious that all guests cannot participate in, nor even observe, the actual ceremony. Therefore it is customary for the close friends and relatives who are to be present for the ceremony to eat last. Others eat and leave. And only after the final serving does the ceremonial activity take place.

The foregoing should not imply that all *makan pulot* are on such a large scale. Many occur throughout the year in Rusembilan in which guests are limited to neighboring villagers and a few relatives and special friends from outside. Not only does the size of the *makan pulot* vary tremendously, but also the specific details of its organization. In celebrating the birthday of the Prophet in 1964, a dozen families in Rusembilan held *makan pulot* serially. To each of these were invited the religious leaders of the village as well as a number of highly respected religious teachers from Islamic schools within Pattani province. Here the ceremonial activities took place before the feast, with religious leaders reciting prayers, and groups of students from the religious schools reading passages from the life of the Prophet. No religious leader went hungry on that day. Whatever its size and however it is specifically organized, each *makan pulot* does function to establish new relationships outside of the community, or at very least to reintensify old ones both inside and beyond the village.

Until quite recently, many people from Rusembilan, before their own rice was ready for harvest, took advantage of the Malayan government's policy of letting temporary laborers into the country at the time of the rice harvest on the west coast. Although agents for many of the larger rice farms in northwestern Malaya are on hand at the railway frontier post, very few of the Malays from South Thailand are recruited by these men. Rather, they will go directly to Malayan villages in which they have a connection. Rarely will this connection be an individual known personally by the villager from South Thailand, but through one or more intermediate steps, in exactly the same manner as invitations to *makan pulot,* the relationship will have been spelled out before the contact and called upon at the time of the visit. The basic reason for employing such network relationships is that it provides for the visitor a feeling of security, and also carries with it a certain set of expectations in regard to hospitality and protection. Furthermore, it often allows the visitor to ignore the purpose for which he was allowed into Malaya in the first place and participate in west coast fishing or in rubber tapping, both occupations which are more congenial. Because of the expansion in the need for labor on the rubber plantations in South Thailand, the practice of taking seasonal employment in Malaya no longer occurs in Rusembilan. Today, men and their wives seek employment as rubber tappers within the country. However, the manner in which they go about it still involves the use of the traditional feasting and marriage relationships that served them in Malaya. The only difference is that working closer to home, there is more likelihood that the contact in the inland village will be firsthand rather than involving intermediate steps.

Purchasing of *kolek* is a matter which traditionally has depended on this same type of relationship. With something as expensive [up to 15,000 *baht* ($750)] as a *kolek,* and where proper design and other less material characteristics are essential for its successful use, it would be unthinkable for a Malay fisherman simply to buy a boat as he would an inexpensive net. It is as important to know the character of the builder and whether he has a "good heart," as it is to be professionally aware of the soundness of the boat. The potential buyer seeks to establish, or activate, a kin or ceremonially based relationship with the builder. Not only does this assure the buyer of the character and reliability of the builder, but it also serves in the other direction to obligate the builder to put his best effort into the boat. The same principle applies in the purchase of a secondhand boat; it is essential to establish a noncommercial relationship with the seller. The Imam of Rusembilan reaped considerable criticism from the village for his failure to establish or employ such channels in his negotiations for the purchase of the first motor tow boat at Rusembilan in 1956. Although the boat was finally bought in Nakorn Sritamarat, some 150 miles away by sea, there were a number of connections between Rusembilan and villages in the neighborhood of Nakorn which could have been employed for this purpose. In spite of their existence, the Imam negotiated with a Thai businessman and purchased a boat which broke down on the return trip before reaching Rusembilan.

While the more formal kin and ceremonial relationships discussed above are employed in large part by men, women of Malay villages participate in similar types of extracommunity relationships. As was pointed out in the last chapter, by far the most frequent contacts with the market town are through the wives of fishermen, not the fishermen themselves. While such contacts are limited to a small group of dealers and vendors, and are generally in the company of other wives of the same boat crew, they do tend to give the women a somewhat more cosmopolitan daily outlook. Women participate in the *makan pulot* both as hostesses and guests. Although they are kept busier at these occasions than are men, from whom they are ordinarily segregated, they do establish their own relationships and contacts in much the same way as do the men. There is one important difference, however: while there are certain reciprocal obligations built into the kin and ceremonial networks of the men, there are usually no such obligations among women. The exception to this statement is in regard to social occasions following the marriage of a young person from the village. The marriage ceremony, which occurs in the village of the bride, is often followed directly (though it may be some days later) by a "viewing of the bride." At this time under the supervision of female relatives of the bride, women of the groom's village (men also if it is directly following the wedding ceremony) file past the couple and contribute a small amount of money in a special collection box. Viewing of the bride requires reciprocation. During the time that the new couple are residing in the groom's village, his female relatives hold a "viewing of the groom" to which women from the bride's village are invited. Light refreshments are served by the groom's relatives, and the women from the bride's village make their small contribution for seeing the groom. There are no further formal obligations involved here, but relationships of importance to the new couple have been clearly indicated, relationships which through employment may acquire certain obligations. Furthermore, lasting relationships between many individuals of the two groups of village women are usually established wherein the channel is a direct one rather than involving the new couple as intermediary.

In the past, more importantly than today, women from Rusembilan and nearby villages were afforded another opportunity to establish and to renew extracommunity relationships by means of the Thursday market in Pattani. Each day of the week except Friday, the Sabbath, market is held in a particular village or small town of Pattani province, and on Thursday the cycle is completed by holding the market in the capital town. In the smaller centers, market day is of considerable economic importance, completely overshadowing any permanent local buying and selling facilities. It is on this day only that produce and goods not ordinarily obtainable locally can be easily purchased by the remote villager. In Pattani, however, with its large municipal market and many shopkeepers and dealers of one sort or another, the Thursday market has little if any important economic function to serve. It was, rather, mainly a focus for social gathering. Women from surrounding villages would dress in their finest clothes, quickly attend to their sales in the main market area, and proceed to the site of the Thursday market some 4 blocks away. Here the women would attend to their daily shopping needs (although the goods were no better nor cheaper than in the municipal market) constantly on the look-out for friends from other villages. It was a gay, festive occasion on which women from many different villages could congregate once a week to gossip and compare ideas on a variety of village activities. With the growth of the town of Pattani, the area surrounding the site of the Thursday market is being rapidly built up with the stores of small merchants, and it provides a secondary center for daily market activities away from the main municipal market. Although this market area now functions continuously, Thursday is still its most important day. Women still come here from the villages to gossip and talk, but much of the festive, social flavor has had to be sacrificed to the increasing commercial importance of the market place.

Through these various channels of relationship, discussed above, a definite pattern of interconnection among the villages of the Pattani area and beyond emerges. Within this pattern, or network, individuals can move throughout the area with almost the same degree of security and set of expectations as they enjoy in their own villages. Also through this same network flows effectively and rapidly the stream of communication linking even remote inland villages through remarkably accurate information with the rest of the area and the outside. Such channels of information play an important part in maintaining social control, to be considered in the next chapter. They are, however, incapable of being exploited for the purposes of the formal Thai government hierarchy operating at the provincial, district, and even local level.

4

Maintaining Control

The "Good Man" and His Influence

TWO ESSENTIALLY different systems of authority appear to be operating in the Malay-speaking area of South Thailand. While there is only very rarely any overlap in the systems themselves or the personnel exercising the authority, there is a significant area of overlap in the units over which this authority is exercised. One system of authority is based directly on the Royal Thai Government and affects the Malay villages and villagers as territorial units within and citizens of the Thai nation. This system of authority will be discussed in the last two sections of this chapter. The other system of authority, which is far more significant in the daily lives of the villagers, is indigenous, and stems directly from the social organization of the Malay communities, based on the traditional and religious values of the villagers. The latter type of authority generally operates unchallenged at the village level; it is at the intercommunity or regional level that it comes into marked conflict with that stemming from Bangkok.

Within the community there are few explicitly defined roles of authority, yet there are individuals whose right to exercise authority and leadership is rarely if ever questioned. These men, *orang baik* ["(morally) good men"] are the respected elders of the community. They are men who through experience, skill, good judgment, and generosity have come to be sought out for their advice and leadership on a wide range of problems. First and foremost they must have a good heart, being kind, helpful, wise, judiciously generous. In short, it can be said that these men most perfectly exemplify the adult values which parents strive to instill into their children (see Chapter 6). Achieving the status of *orang baik* is an imperceptible transition. It has a good deal to do with the number and frequency of requests for advice or assistance. Often it is easier for a man in a position of authority in economic matters, such as a boat owner or, more so, a steerer to achieve this status. These men exercise authority in their economic roles and people are accustomed to seeking their advice. *Orang baik* are accorded general respect by the community: they are spoken to first on meeting, they are among those who are invited to almost every *makan pulot* in their villages, and to many outside, and when in need of assistance themselves, they are given aid generously by many in the community.

Respect is also marked by the use of titles. The most respectful of these is *tok,* "grandfather." In Rusembilan this title is not used for anyone except the Imam whose formal status, rather than personal qualities, determines its use. The kin-derived terms *pak* and *pachu* have been discussed in the previous chapter. It is the group of men called *pak* who generally comprise the *orang baik* of the community. If a man reaches old age without having achieved a position of respect marked by one of these titles, he is usually given the title *wak,* "old man," signifying respect for his age. In addition to these titles of respect, there also occur in the Malay villages of South Thailand formal titles of connection with one or another of the royal families formerly in the region. Like other areas of Southeast Asia, such titles are not absolute, in that as relationships shade off from the ruling line either by degrees of collaterality or over generations, the status of the relative and therefore the titles are degraded, until after seven steps of remove, commoner status is reached. In Rusembilan this system of degrading is not followed. However, titles connected with royalty do not carry much significance either. People would prefer, if appropriate, to be addressed by a title of meaningful respect.

In any community with its individuals, their various interests and different motivations, there are bound to be conflicts, breeches of the orderly pattern of events, or simply decisions to be made concerning unusual problems or situations confronting the community as a whole. It is at these times that the *orang baik* come together as a formal body to deliberate action. Often, a dispute is settled or a decision made by one of these men alone; sometimes two or three of them will sit in a coffee shop, or in the shade of a coconut tree and discuss the community's problems with interested villagers. Rarely does there appear to be any formal or deliberate action taken. In the event that a villager is confronted by any unusual situation, problem, or dispute, he will first seek the advice of whichever of these respected men he feels most familiar with. Often the solution is suggested almost at once. However, further consultation may be necessary, the initiative for which can be taken either by the villager with his problem or by the *orang baik.* Sometimes when the problem has religious implications (as do many) the Imam is consulted or one of the several other respected religious leaders in the community. Because of his formal and official position in the village it is usually the Imam who decides whether a particularly difficult problem can, in fact, be solved within the community, or whether it must be brought to the attention of the Thai governmental authorities. This decision need not be based on criteria which would meet the approval of the government—as a matter of fact many situations legally calling for government action are handled entirely within the community. Theft, which is a matter legally requiring the attention of the Pattani police, is handled, whenever possible, entirely within the community or between two communities. Identification of the culprit generally presents no grave problems, for most villagers are well aware of the activities of their neighbors and information travels quickly. Once the thief has been identified, he is usually approached by an *orang baik* and lectured in terms of traditional and Islamic values. This is equally true of the thief who hails from another Malay village, as through their more numerous and frequent kin and ceremonial-type relationships *orang baik* in one village are apt to be in close contact with those in another. In many cases such lectures by respected men in the community result in restitution of the stolen article. Sometimes they do not. In the latter case, the victim of the theft may be advised to seek reprisal on his own— simply by reclaiming the stolen article if he can, or by taking something of equal value from the thief. The system works amazingly well, for it has the weight of public opinion and particularly that of the respected members of the community behind it. Occasionally, because of the magnitude of the crime or the incorrigibility of the culprit, the case must eventually be taken to government authorities and to court litigation. Rarely, one or the other of the parties may be dissatisfied with the outcome and the dispute may be continued on for many years as a smoldering feud, flaring up from time to time in actual violence.

An incident which occurred during the summer of 1964 illustrates the point that the largely informal authority within the community does not always work. Two young men of Rusembilan had the previous year cooperated in building a small boat. On completion of the boat a dispute arose over its ownership, one claiming that it was entirely his because he had provided all the materials going into it, the other claiming specific rights to use the boat because of the time and labor he had contributed. Neither man was satisfied with the decision reached through consultation with respected elders; that the boat be shared, but not to an extent acceptable to the man contributing labor alone. Throughout the year hard feelings and occasional minor fights characterized the relationship between these two men. Finally, as one was sitting on the ground sawing a piece of wood, the other, coming from behind, drew his *parang* (a long heavy knife with hooked point) and slashed a 5-inch wound above the eye of the first. The wounded man was rushed to the government hospital where he remained for two weeks recovering from shock and the wound. Several points emerged from this incident in regard to authority in the village. The first, as mentioned, is that the solutions arrived at by informal leaders are not always acceptable. Villagers, for whom this was a major subject of gossip for some time, pointed out that the whole situation would never have occurred had these two men not been from families in which traditional and Islamic values were not sufficiently emphasized. Neither of these men had "good hearts," which was directly attributable to their upbringing. To further drive home the point, it was constantly mentioned that the brother of one of the men had "always fought" and as a final desperate resort his parents had enrolled him in religious school to keep him out of trouble.

It is required by the government that any fight resulting in injury to the face must be reported immediately to the police, that it is a crime requiring their attention and prosecution. Villagers were well aware of this requirement, and not surprised to find the police in Rusembilan even before the party taking the victim to the hospital had returned to the village. The assailant, of course, had fled and taken refuge elsewhere as soon as he had committed his violent act. Because it was considered by the villagers that this situation belonged properly within the sphere of community authority, even though it had not found suitable resolution by this means, no one offered the police any information either about the nature of the dispute or about the identity or whereabouts of the assailant. While it is possible that the culprit could have remained undetected by the authorities (in many cases this happens) it was felt eventually by the *orang baik* of Rusembilan that the nature of the case was such that they could no longer handle it internally. Therefore they counseled the young man to report to the police and ask for leniency. This he did. It is uncertain what the outcome of this incident will be—theoretically it must be prosecuted in the district court, with a probable result of three to five years in prison. More likely, if funds can be obtained, it can be settled out of court, that is, the court authorities can be persuaded to remove the whole incident from the records.

Another recent dispute stemmed from a divorce case. This, of course, involved two different villages. The woman, on being divorced by her husband, had returned to Rusembilan, her home village, bringing with her a six-month old son, but leaving with her husband in his village a boy of two. This was considered right and proper by all who discussed the matter in Rusembilan. However, the husband thought that he should have custody of both children. As his requests for the baby were to no avail, he simply came to Rusembilan one night and kidnapped the child. Resistance was not offered as the husband had brought with him two friends armed with pistols. Although matters involving marriage and divorce are ordinarily within the realm of the Imam, it was felt that in this instance traditional values were more strongly on the side of the woman than were Islamic values, and further that the former husband would be more responsive to social than to religious pressure. Thus a group of *orang baik* in Rusembilan considered the matter, and finally took it to a comparable group in the husband's village. Most of these men were personally known to one another, for there had been several marriage alliances between the two villages, as well as considerable interchange of invitations for *makan pulot*. The discussions between the elders of the two villages resulted in agreement that the baby should be returned to his mother, at least until it was less dependent on her care (at this point she was still nursing it—when she had the opportunity). The *orang baik* of the other village talked severally with the husband and eventually persuaded him to return the child to its mother.

A number of disputes flared up at Rusembilan with the introduction of motor tow boats. It is only necessary here to mention the role of the *orang baik* in this situation. The crisis was brought about in the first place by the inability of these men to reach a generally agreed upon and clear-cut policy regarding the course of progress in the fishing industry. This was due in part to the fact that most of the *orang baik* were personally involved in the decision as to whether to go ahead and acquire tow boats. They lacked the detachment and objectivity characteristic of their authority in other matters. When conflict erupted over inability to cooperate properly as members of a three-*kolek* tow group, the *orang baik* were similarly unable to take decisive action. Ultimately, on the initiative of one of these men, Rusembilan started ridding itself of the tow boats and outfitting each *kolek* with outboard motors.

Perhaps one of the most significant measures directed at community control by the *orang baik* of Rusembilan was the organization of a village patrol system to operate on those nights when the majority of village men were at sea. On three or four occasions in 1956, thieves broke into Rusembilan homes. These thieves belonged to an organized group which was robbing villages throughout the area and were not responsive to community or even intercommunity authority. Government police protection was requested by Rusembilan, but the police, busy with other matters and other areas, could not comply. It was therefore decided by the majority of steerers and boat owners of Rusembilan (most of whom were *orang baik*) that each *kolek* crew would leave one member ashore every fishing night. These men would receive their full share of fish as payment for their patrol duties. The village was divided into a number of districts, and the men patrolling in pairs, either for company or so that they might take turns sleeping, allocated themselves to whatever district they chose. While there was some difficulty caused by the individual assignment of districts, the patrol operated successfully, completely stopping crimes in Rusembilan, in spite of a rising crime rate in other areas of the province. Had the community patrol not involved roles based on boat crew membership, and specifically boat crew authority, it would probably not have functioned so successfully nor so continuously.

There is often a measure of outside coersion involved in organizing community projects. The coersion may be as mild as an order from the district officer, for the villagers of Rusembilan and other Malay villages have traditionally been subject to *corvee* labor, and expect it. The case of the visit of the Queen Mother to Pattani, mentioned in Chapter 3, is illustrative both of the initiation of such effort from the outside, and also of its internalization (which is not always the case) as a community project. The order which came from the district office made it quite clear that every coastal village in the district was to provide a boat for the flotilla, it further indicated that the boats were to be decorated. Many of the boats that participated in the flotilla simply met the bare requirements. However, because of the enthusiasm of a relatively young *orang baik* in Rusembilan, there grew a general acceptance of the project as a matter of village pride and competition against other villages. Considerable organization, as well as expense for decorations and costumes, went into outfitting the village boat. Young men had to receive instruction in paddling, a skill which had long since been supplanted by oars, sails, and motors. An orchestra had to be assembled and rehearsed. The boat had to be thoroughly cleaned and painted, and finally a huge crepe paper garuda bird on a framework of wire was to be constructed on the bow. For two weeks the village was the scene of constant discussion and activity under the direction of several interested elders, and at six in the morning of the Queen Mother's arrival, virtually the whole village had turned out to wish their fellow villagers well in their competition against other villages. Great was the rejoicing in the village that evening when the boat returned to Rusembilan triumphantly, having been awarded by the Queen Mother herself the prize (a new sarong for each crew man) for the most beautiful boat.

The *Tambon* and the Village Headman

The Thai term *tambon,* often translated as "commune," refers to the next smallest unit below the district, or *amphur.* To all intents and purposes from the point of view of the hierarchy of officialdom spreading down from Bangkok, the *tambon* is the smallest administrative unit. It is at this level that central government appointees, the district officers, come in contact with locally based officials. That there are legally constituted subunits within the *tambon* and subofficials beneath the *kamnan* (the administrative officer of the *tambon*) is of little practical consequence to the district or provincial administration. Actually the *tambon* is composed of a number of *muban* (in the South these are simply called by the Malay term *kampong,* "village") each with its own administrative officer under the *kamnan.* Tambon Rusembilan contains five *kampong,* one of which consists of the village of Rusembilan together with the satellite hamlets. As far as economic or social intercourse is concerned, the other four *kampong* are separate, unrelated villages, only one of which shares with Rusembilan a predominantly sea-faring orientation.

Traditionally, the *kamnan* has been elected from *kampong* Rusembilan, for this community makes up more than half the total population of the *tambon.* In his job he has been assisted by a deputy headman or secretary, while the other units of the *tambon* have been represented by *naiban* (village heads), subordinate to the *kamnan.* For reasons external to the village situation, the present *kamnan* of Rusembilan is not from the main village, but from a settlement on the border of Pattani municipality. Communication with the district office is facilitated, but the sense of a lack of self-determination in community affairs is heightened for a majority of the population of the *tambon.* The *kamnan* is supposed to be elected by a vote of all male heads of family within the *tambon* from a slate of nominees put up by the villagers and approved by the district officer. Actually, the selection of the new *kamnan* of Rusembilan in 1962 was made somewhat differently. The five *naiban* were called together by the district officer, who allegedly spoke in glowing terms of one of them. The *naiban* were then asked to choose from among themselves one to be *kamnan.* It is not surprising that the man backed by the district officer was selected. Villagers responded to this choice, on the whole, negatively: "the *naiban* from *kampong* Rusembilan would have been *kamnan* if not for the intervention of the district officer"; "the man selected is not the right person [for the job], all the people were not consulted in his selection, but the district officer likes him, and simply announced his appointment." Selection of the *naiban* for each of the component units of the *tambon* is carried out in fact in precisely the same manner as selection of the *kamnan* is in theory, subject always to the approval of the district officer. There is rarely much dissatisfaction among the villagers about their *nai-ban,* and he may even occupy the status of *orang baik.*

Basically the job of the *kamnan* is to keep track of the population in his charge, to inform the district authorities of significant happenings in the village, and to implement policies and orders passed down to him through the district office. Specifically, he must keep as accurate count as possible of births and deaths among the population, likewise he must know the number of cattle in his villages for tax purposes, he is notified of all warrants for arrest within his *tam-bon* and is expected to cooperate fully with the police, he must accompany to the district office and vouch for villagers applying for permits to buy land or slaughter cattle; see that they pay their taxes, and convoke the increasingly rare village meetings. Once a month all *kamnan* from the district meet with the district officer who generally lectures to them on good government and the importance of concern with the well-being of the people. The meeting also serves as a means of making known to the *kamnan* the orders which the district officer wants carried out, and also for informing the district officer of happenings in the villages. The *naiban's* duties are parallel to those of the *kamnan* but on a smaller scale. In addition, he usually has the respect of the villagers and finds his tasks therefore somewhat easier to perform. Far more of the *naiban's* time is consumed with listening to complaints or to requests for government services from the villagers. However, by the time these have filtered up to the district officer they have usually lost most of their urgency.

In 1956, the villagers of Rusembilan were generally dissatisfied with their *kamnan,* feeling he was simply a "yes-man" for the district officer, and negligent in his duty to the village. A number of men joined together in the coffee shops to discuss the possibilities of having this man removed from office, for it is theoretically possible to take such action in the case of manifest incompetence. They specifically felt that the *kamnan* was "weak," and that he feared to speak for the villagers to the district officer. This agitation came to nought, however, as most influential men in the village felt it was more prudent not to curry trouble with the district office. After holding the position of *kamnan* for twenty-three years, this man finally died, and was replaced by his assistant who was a well-respected man in Rusembilan, a brother of *Pak Sa.* Even this man had difficulty in retaining the sympathies of the villagers, as an important part of the job of *kamnan* is the implementation of government orders in the villages. It was with considerable embarrassment, however, that the villagers complained of their new *kamnan* in 1960. As this man did represent the true leadership of Rusembilan, it would have been interesting to observe how he eventually reconciled the conflicts inherent in his role. It is unfortunate, therefore, that he was killed in an automobile accident in 1962. At that time, the present *kamnan* was selected and, as he was not a local leader, complaints again became loud and open in the village.

One of the most unpopular tasks which the *kamnan* must perform is gathering together members of the community (usually men) to undertake village projects requested by the district office. In Rusembilan, until 1964, maintenance of the village road was the most common occasion for such work groups. Even during the "dry" seasons of the year the frequent rain storms turn the major portion of the mile and a half long village road into a sea of mud with numerous deep puddles which completely prohibit the passage of motor traffic. As delivery of fuel for the village's outboard motors, construction materials for new houses, and the daily bus must be able to get into Rusembilan, it is imperative that the road be maintained. Essentially what the village men were called on to do periodically, aside from keeping culverts in repair, was to shovel up more mud from the rice fields along the road in order to decrease the depth of the puddles and ruts. Coconut husks would be thrown into the worst of these and often the whole thing would be topped with fronds fallen from coconut trees, giving an illusion of firmness. This was arduous work, and in the past confined to Friday mornings before services in the mosque because, until recently, the fishermen of Rusembilan did not go to sea Thursday night—the Sabbath running from sunset Thursday until sunset Friday. With falling fish prices and sharper competition, the fishermen finally decided, in spite of protests by the Imam, that they must fish on Thursday. Therefore they resented even more strenuously being called on to fill holes in the road on Friday morning. As a consequence the road deteriorated to a point where the bus was sometimes unable to reach the village. At that point the owner of the bus (a Thai woman) took matters in her own hands and hired a villager for 100 *baht* ($5.00) a month to keep the road passable. The fate of this arrangement is uncertain.

Among the other projects for which the *kamnan* must conscript village labor is that of keeping free of silt the various estuary channels of the Pattani River within the *tambon*. Villagers say that salt water backs up into their rice fields through these channels during the monsoon tides. On several occasions they have refused to participate in the desilting operation. When this happens, a wise *kamnan* simply lets the matter drop. In 1956, Rusembilan was granted funds for the construction of a new primary school building, and for this project village labor was also required. Unlike the labor recruited for the construction of private houses, reciprocal obligations played no part in this. The best that the *kamnan* could arrange was for the women of the village to prepare food for the workers. However, after a large turnout of men the first day, resulting in the building and erection of wall and roof frameworks, work virtually ceased. The women could not be asked to provide food more than once and a large labor force was no longer needed. A small group of men with appropriate skills was needed over a period of time to complete the job. Those men who could be persuaded to work did not possess the skills which were required. Consequently, the roof was covered with clay tiles before the walls had been boarded, in fact, before the wall frameworks had been properly braced. After the collapse of the top-heavy uncompleted building one evening during a wind storm and the serious injury to a child who was playing within, it proved somewhat easier to get village men to work on, and finally complete, a second and somewhat smaller school building.

Among the *kamnan's* duties is assembling as many of the village heads of households as he can for periodic meetings with the district officer. In 1956 the district officer felt it advisable to hold such meetings roughly once every three months, in order to bring to the attention of the villagers some aspects of government policy broader than the orders sent down through the *kamnan,* and to listen to complaints, comments, and suggestions of the villagers. While this was an admirable plan for improving relations between the village and the district, it failed to work for a number of reasons. Although attendance at the meetings was compulsory, rarely did more than a third of the household heads of Rusembilan appear. Their reason was that they had not been notified of the meeting sufficiently in advance. Communication at the meetings was decidedly one way—they tended to be lectures given by the district officer. The villagers, ordinarily full of complaints and suggestions, reasoned that if they voiced their opinions the best they could hope for was that they would be ignored. The language problem also rendered these meetings of little value to anyone. The district officer spoke only Thai, the villagers understood only Malay. It was the job of the *kamnan,* or the village school teacher if he were available, to translate. However, the *kamman's* command of Thai was as limited as the school teacher's command of Malay, so usually only about a quarter of what was said got translated, and most of that incorrectly. Subsequent district officers, realizing these obstacles to communication with the villagers, have given up the idea of periodic village meetings, holding them only in cases where important government announcements must be taken to the villagers rapidly. In these cases they now supply their own translators.

A government order in 1956 required that each *tambon* in the nation create a village council of elected representatives to assist the *kamnan* in carrying out some of his duties and to bring a sense of democratic self-government and national awareness to all the villagers of Thailand. The council would meet at least once a year to discuss matters of village importance such as protection, welfare, building, and development projects. A special meeting with the district officer was called in Rusembilan to create such a council. Although the villagers present at the meeting were asked for nominations, none spoke. Finally the *kamnan* suggested a group of men and asked for village approval. Again the villagers remained silent, and with the assent of the district officer, the *kamnan's* nominees were appointed. The villagers, when asked why they had made no nominations of their own, had replied, "it would have done no good, as all nominations must be approved by the *kamnan* and the district office. The men chosen were all men that the *kamnan* could count on. The only result will be that there are now more officials in the village to call us out for work projects." It is uncertain whether this council ever functioned in Rusembilan; it was not functioning in 1960 nor in 1964. There is certainly no desire on the part of the villagers to activate it, and the present district administration appears to have adopted a policy of not forcing on the villages organizations which they do not want. In inland villages of the area, however, these village councils have evolved into a basic local unit in the government's community development scheme, and will be considered briefly as such in Chapter 7.

So far all dealings of villagers with the government hierarchy represented by the district office have been treated in terms of the *kamman.* This is by far the most important channel. But there are other minor contacts the village has with the government. The most dramatic of these is when the district police descend on the village upon hearing of a crime. They are supposed to receive the full cooperation of the *kamnan,* but in many cases, pleading the importance of time, the police do not even bother to notify the *kamnan* of crimes committed in his *tambon.* The school provides another area of contact between the villagers and the district and provincial educational authorities: this will be considered in some detail in Chapter 6. The only other area of contact is in regard to medical and health matters. In cases of emergency villagers do not hesitate to call on the facilities of the government hospital in Pattani, although when time and distance are not important they prefer to seek assistance at the missionary hospital in Saiburi. Provincial health officials visit Rusembilan and other villages in the province every other year to spray dwellings with DDT as a malaria control measure. In addition, each *tambon* has its appointed medical officer. In Rusembilan, this man is one of the two village *bomo* (shaman), who is less averse to acting as liaison between the village and the government medical services in which he believes (for certain types of malady) than he is to donning a government uniform to attend along with the *kamnan* the monthly meetings at the district office. The function of this village medical officer is to see that people who need medical attention receive it, and to certify all births and deaths in the *tambon,* and to notify the *kamnan* of such statistics.

As has been stated or implied throughout this section, relations between the Malay villagers and the district officials are not generally cordial. Occasionally, a highly motivated man who knows or learns the Malay language is appointed district officer, and relations in his district improve for the period he remains in office. Ordinarily, like the provincial officers, the district officer is a Thai from another part of the country who has no interest and little knowledge of the special problems confronting the government in Malay-speaking provinces, and who is only concerned with accomplishing his job with as little trouble as possible and being transferred to a more pleasant assignment. The villagers for their part have come to suspect the intentions and policies of all Thais, and do little if anything to improve relationships with that part of the national government which impinges most directly on them.

District, *Changwat,* and Nation

T. J. Newbold, writing of the Malay state of Pattani (Malayan and British spelling, Patani) in 1839, gives the following brief account of the period when Siam (Thailand) ultimately gained political control over this area:

> Patani . . . was conquered by Siam about 1603 A.D., again about 1786, and finally, in 1832. The Rajah [of Pattani] fled to Kalantan [sic], but was given up, and is now a state prisoner in Siam. His country has been heavily taxed; many of its inhabitants made slaves, and numbers carried away into captivity to Siam. The Praklang [military commander] took with him from Patani to Bangkok, in September, 1832, upwards of four thousand captives, in a dreadful state of misery (Newbold 1839: Vol. II, Ch. 7).

One hundred years later the Malay inhabitants of the former kingdom, now divided into the three provinces of Pattani, Yala, and Narathiwat, still kept alive the memory (if not the details) of this period. Indeed, to their way of thinking, matters had not improved significantly. It was in 1939 that the Pibun government took its first aggressive steps toward integration of minority groups, leading directly to the "cultural rules" of 1940. Under these rules it was required that all citizens of Thailand dress in western clothes, including brimmed hats, that they eat with fork and spoon sitting on chairs at a table, that they refrain from chewing betel nut, and that they could no longer carry loads on their heads. Furthermore, the use of the Malay language was outlawed, as was the practice of Islam. Fines were imposed for infractions of these rules, and in the case of clothing infractions, garments were frequently ripped off and trampled by the enforcing officials. Although the cultural rules were repealed shortly after the end of World War II, neither the memory of them, nor the attitude of many Thai officials who had been in charge of enforcing them died quickly. The situation has not been helped by a vacillation of government policy since that time in the degree of concession toward Malay cultural, religious, and linguistic autonomy in the four southern provinces.

This is the background against which to place the efforts of officials at the district, provincial, and national levels to find solutions to the administrative problems in the South. Thailand today is divided into seventy-one *changwat* or provinces, each administered by a governor responsible to the Minister of Internal Affairs. At the provincial level each governor is assisted by a staff of officials representing the functional ministries and departments of the central government. The province itself is further subdivided into districts, or *amphur,* of which there are eight in Pattani province. The district officer, *nai amphur,* the administrative head of this unit is directly subordinate to the governor. In his administration he is assisted by a number (depending on the size and importance of the district) of district-level functional officials who are directly subordinate to their provincial counterparts as well as being under the supervisory control of the district officer. With minor variations this system has been in effect in Malay-speaking areas of South Thailand since 1901 or 1902. The large majority of these civil servants are Thai-speaking Buddhists (under the cultural rules they had to be) hailing from other regions of the country. It is the policy of the Ministry of Internal Affairs to rotate its officers fairly frequently to minimize the danger of their establishing close ties with local individuals or institutions which might tend to impede efficiency and impartiality of government administration.

In Pattani town, seat of both provincial and district administrations, offices and other government buildings are located across the river from the main part of the town. There is little else on this side of the river. It is almost a mile from the municipal market and villagers and others have relatively little contact with the physical presence of these two levels of government unless they have specific business to conduct there. Perhaps the most common form of business the ordinary villager has at the government offices is the payment of his taxes.

Like conscripted labor for community projects, the Malay villager realizes that taxation is necessary in order to finance the government services from which he benefits. However, as with *corvee* labor for projects of which he disapproves, the villager is not happy at the thought of paying for government services which he either does not see or feels are not necessary. Cultivated land in the villages is taxed at a rate of 1½ *baht* per *rai* (about 18 cents per acre in 1956) while unused lands are taxed at only two thirds of this rate. In addition, the villager of Rusembilan is charged an annual registration tax on his *kolek* (smaller boats are exempt), license fees for selling cigarettes and kerosene, and for the slaughter of cattle. All in all, a village the size of Rusembilan probably does not contribute much more than 5000 *baht* ($250) to an annual provincial income of some five hundred times that much. It is the responsibility of the taxpayer to see that his tax is paid at the district office when it is due. The *kamnan* of each *tambon* should notify the taxpayers of this date, but even if he does not, it is the taxpayers who are responsible and who are subject to fines (and eventually confiscation for delinquency). Registration in the national census is a means whereby the local and central government can assess its resources and obligations in terms of population. Villagers are registered by representatives of the district office at ten-year intervals. Failure to register is punished by denial of the privileges of changing residence, buying land, and of leaving the country (most importantly, undertaking the pilgrimage to Mecca)—in short, of basic rights of citizenship.

In one other obligation to the state, the villager is regularly brought into contact with the district administration. Annually, each male who has reached the age of twenty-one within the past year is called to the district office for the national-service draft. Prior to this, on his eighteenth birthday, a young man must register for the draft, but it is especially at the time of conscription that he feels most acutely his relationship with the state. Although only a few names are drawn from the bowl in any district, the conscription proceedings is a time of great anxiety for the Malay youth and his family. Whenever possible the parents will have paid to have their son's name removed from the rolls; however, this is costly and few can afford it. These young men are extremely upset at the idea of being placed in a military training camp among Thais and far from their own homes and relatives. This is of course compounded by the fact that most of the Malay youths do not speak Thai, and by the fact that Muslim dietary laws do not obtain, nor are they recognized, in the Thai army.

Law and the administration of justice are areas of state control in which there are important cultural differences between the Thai and Malays. As was mentioned earlier, when these matters can be confined to the local, village level, they are dealt with in terms of traditional or Islamic practice or both. However, when a Malay villager is brought into the Thai civil courts he is at a severe disadvantage. In recognition of this, the government in the past allowed Islamic courts to operate alongside of the civil courts for cases dealing with marriage, divorce, and property settlement, all matters involving Islamic law. During the period of the cultural rules, Islamic courts along with the profession of Islam itself were outlawed, throwing the villager squarely into the Thai legal system and the civil courts. More recent government policy has required that civil courts be staffed with two Thai-Malay interpreters who must translate all proceedings into both languages. In addition, each judge presiding in a case involving Muslims must have present at all times a Muslim advisor of equivalent civil service rank as himself. The advisor counsels the judge on matters bearing on Islamic law and belief and also on matters of Malay tradition. Although the judge is under no obligation to accept this advice, it is effective in many cases.

The structure of the recently introduced Thai community development program exactly parallels the hierarchy of administrative government, at least down to the *amphur* level. The major difference, however, is that the whole program is aimed at helping the villagers of Thailand, so that contacts between the government officials and the villagers tend to be more frequent, and of necessity more positively received by the villager. For, in spite of a number of serious blunders on the part of the government, it is obvious to the villager that the program as well as the specific projects have been conceived for his benefit. Although community development operations had not yet been extended to the coastal districts of Pattani province by 1964, villagers at Rusembilan were aware of the program. In fact, they hoped that the ultimate solution to some of their economic problems might be brought about through this agency. High on their list of problems which they hoped the government might be able to solve for them was their belief that large-scale commercial netting operations in the Gulf of Thailand were taking young as well as mature fish indiscriminately. It was hoped that the government might fix and enforce regulations regarding the minimum mesh size of nets for various species of fish and areas of operation.

Although the Thai government through such efforts as community development is making a sincere effort to help the people of the South (as well as other areas of the country), and although the people of the South realize this, there are still large areas of misunderstanding and hard feeling between Thais and Malays of the area. Some of these and the historical bases for their existence have already been sketched. The linguistic problem is one of the chief sources of difficulty between the two groups of people in the South, but it is only one of them. The official 1960 census figures indicate that 37 percent of the population of Pattani speaks Thai. This would be somewhat under 30 percent of the indicated Muslim population. It is probable that even this figure is misleadingly high and represents at most the knowledge of a handful of Thai words of little practical value. Efforts are being made to improve the situation by developing intensive instructional methods in the Thai language for use in primary and religious schools. These efforts and some of the obstacles to be met will be discussed in Chapter 6. On the other hand, the Thai government is presently encouraging its servants at all ranks to acquire proficiency in Malay. Malay word lists appear regularly in the Thai language newspaper published in Haad Yai, and short, intensive training camps in Malay language and culture have been set up for Thai officials, with the understanding that on passing a proficiency test in the Malay language the official will be entitled to a regular salary bonus.

A far more deep-rooted part of the problem, however, involves the attitudes held by one group in regard to the other. While the majority of Thais and Malays having dealings with one another may be men of good will, the existence of prejudice on the part of even a small minority may have serious effects on the course of intergroup relations in South Thailand. Two illustrations will suffice to demonstrate that prejudice against the Malays is still present among government officials in the South of Thailand. In making a routine check of *kolek* registrations, a police corporal was unable to locate the owner of a particular boat he was checking. The man's wife answered the policeman's questions, giving all the requisite information. However, the policeman did not consider this sufficient and demanded to see the registration certificate. The woman said that she would get it from the house, but the police officer demanded that he accompany her. This he did with considerable noise and indignation. Moreover, he marched into the house wearing his heavy patrol boots—a serious breech of etiquette in either a Thai or a Malay house. The other illustration concerns remarks made by one of the highest-ranking provincial officials at an important state dinner given by the governor. This official indicated that he considered the Malays to be an inferior race, and essentially stupid. He questioned the efforts being made in the South to increase the number of Malay children attending school, feeling that they "could not be educated," or even if they could it would only mean that they would be more troublesome for the government.

Even without such open prejudice, there is a common tendency among many Thai officials stationed in the South to assume a superior attitude in dealings with village peoples (this is not entirely confined to the South). The Thais encountered by Malay villagers are almost always better educated than the villagers themselves, and as it is not uncommon to equate intelligence with educational level, it is hardly surprising that a sense of inferiority and superiority with attendant graft and exploitation finds itself into such cross-cultural relationships. There is a saying among Thais in the South, which has achieved almost the status of a proverb, that "a government officer who has no money is stupid."

The Malays of South Thailand realize quite well what their position is and, remembering the past war years, how serious it can become. They emphatically insist on their right to maintain their cultural, linguistic, and religious distinctiveness. At times this actually becomes an insistence on political distinctiveness. This is equally true of villager as it is of educated Muslim leader. In the words of one man of Rusembilan, "Thailand is not our country—it is over there (pointing toward Malaysia). We are Malays, not Thai Islam." The term Thai Islam is an invention of the Thai government to indicate that while it does tolerate religious differences now, it does not consider that there should be any other significant differences among citizens of Thailand. In 1947, Haji Sulong, an important leader among the Malays of Pattani, said in an address:

We Malays are conscious that we have been brought under Siamese rule by defeat. The term "Thai Islam" with which we are known by the Siamese government reminds us of this defeat and is therefore not appreciated by us. We therefore beg of the government to honour us with the title of Malay Muslims so that we may be recognized as distinct from the Thai by the outside world. (Quoted in *Annals of Pattani.*)

The attitude of the Malay villager toward Malaysia is strongly positive. However, his knowledge of the country is scanty. Most of the twelve radios in

Rusembilan are tuned in on Radio Malaysia, although the people of South Thailand can understand the Kuala Lumper dialect of Malay only with difficulty. Villagers have the greatest respect for Tungku Abdul Rahman, Prime Minister of Malaysia, "he is leading his nation according to the principles of Islam." As would be expected, the greater the degree of actual or imagined oppression by the Thai government and its representatives in the South, the greater is the Malay villager's positive attitude toward the Malayan nation to the South. On several occasions this has led to rather large-scale irredentist movements and uprisings in the provinces of Pattani, Yala, and Narathiwat.[1]

While there is no dearth of leadership for such movements within the Thai provinces, at least some of the instigation has come from political parties across the border in the Malaysian state of Kelantan. The scope of such movements and uprisings and the exact details of their courses of events are difficult data to obtain objectively. It is generally agreed that at one point or another some 250,000 Malays have been more or less actively involved in such movements, and that the suppressive measures of the Thai police, sometimes aided by the army, have on occasion been more extreme than was necessary.

In an effort to work out a peaceful solution to the difficulties in South Thailand, while at the same time retaining the area as Thai territory, the following seven-point program was proposed to the government by a group of Muslim leaders, including Haji Sulong. First, the governors of the four Malay provinces should be local men chosen by the residents of the provinces involved and should serve an indefinite term of office. Second, all revenue received from this area should be used for improvements within the area (the South is important both for exportable rubber and tin). Third, Malay education should be permitted at least for the first four years of primary school. Fourth, at least 80 percent of the civil service positions in the area should be filled by Malays local to the area. Fifth, the Malay language should be allowed along with Thai for the transaction of official business. Sixth and seventh, religious courts must be separate from civil authority in religious matters and the Muslim Religious Board should be allowed to issue rules, subject to the approval of the governors, relating to matters in which Islamic law is concerned. These demands were obviously all not met. However, certain concessions have been made by the government; several of them have been mentioned previously. Specifically, the government ruled that Friday should be the legal holiday in Muslim areas rather than Sunday as in other parts of the kingdom; the government-controlled radio was allowed to devote a portion of its air time to Malay language and music broadcasts; and a program was undertaken to expand as rapidly as possible modern educational facilities for the Malays. Of these three concessions granted, only one has since been rescinded: the legal holiday is once again Sunday.

Although political parties have been outlawed throughout Thailand since 1958, at one point these provided an outlet for some of the Malays' feelings of oppression and hostility. The government, in 1956, recognized that a political

---

[1] Advocating the secession of and reincorporation of a portion of one nation into another; here advocating the union of the Malay-speaking provinces of Thailand with Malaya.

party was potentially dangerous in such a situation, but felt, probably with justification, that recognizing them as such would tend to keep them in the open, and that much destructive energy could be channeled into constructive or at least neutral campaigning. In 1956 there was high interest even in remote villages over the election to be held early in 1957. Candidates, both Thai and Malay, swept into villages in festooned jeeps, distributing gifts and making wild promises. The fact that no one really took the promises seriously did not matter. It was a festive time, and temporarily, chronic discontents were forgotten. It is significant that in the two previous elections in Thailand only 10 percent and 39 percent of the eligible voters in the nation participated, while in Pattani province 126,725 votes were recorded in the 1957 election out of a *total* population which in 1960 was just over 280,000.

5

Dealing with the Supernatural

Spirits, Illness, and the *Bomo*

WHEN GOD CREATED Adam and Eve, Satan, still in good favor, was granted his request for immortality and unlimited fertility. Even after his expulsion from Paradise and the destruction of his magnificent heavenly palaces on account of his deception of the first human couple, Satan retained his gifts, and in addition, was granted the power to deceive all those who neglected to follow the Law of God. In his work since that time, Satan has created a vast number of offspring to assist in his deceptions. Like their progenitor, these beings are immortal. However, they do share with man the power of choice between good and evil. These beings are the *jin Islam,* recognized by the Koran, and by extension include also another large category of traditonal Malay spirits, by nature malevolent, the *hantu.*

In addition to this joint class of spirits, there is a special category of supernatural force which Rusembilan and the Malays of South Thailand share in greater or lesser degree with most of the Malayo-Polynesian language groups of Southeast Asia. This is *semangat,* a soul-substance or vital force found in all things. Its quantity, and perhaps quality, vary from object to object and from one part of an object to another. However, whether resident in inanimate objects, plants, animals, or men it is the same. In Rusembilan, there is some confusion between *semangat* and the mortal soul of man. Villagers feel that it may leave the body of a person during dreams, and that therefore it is most dangerous to awaken suddenly a soundly sleeping man, for he might wake without his *semangat* which would then have no way of returning. In this same vein, the villagers believe that *semangat* ceases to exist with the death of its possessor, whether animate or inanimate. However, in the manner of the concept elsewhere in Southeast Asia, a man may recharge his supply of *semangat* by contact with or, better, incorporation of some highly charged object. Legendary men, as well as present-day *hantu,* are wont to recharge their supplies of *semangat* by contact with that object having the greatest concentration of it, the human head —particularly that of an illustrious man. Malay villagers, violently eschewing the idea of cannibalism or head-hunting themselves, do recognize both its utility and its practice by evil spirits. The villagers substitute *nasi semangat,* a specially prepared ceremonial rice, as their means of renewing this spiritual force. *Nasi semangat* is a part of most important ceremonial activities in these villages; it can never be absent from those celebrating the life crises. These are dangerous periods in the life of the individual, his or her relatives, and by extension, the whole community. Therefore, it is necessary to bolster the group of participants with as much *semangat* as possible.

The loss of *semangat,* or its insufficiency, is usually manifested by poor crops, infertility of women, generally run-down conditions in the village, and illness. None of these conditions is exclusively attributable to the loss of *semangat* so that when one occurs a problem of diagnosis is presented. This is one of the roles of the *bomo,* to be discussed below. However, in any event it does no harm to attempt to build up *semangat* at these times, and it is essential to do so at certain decisive points as a means of insurance. Rejuvenation of *semangat* to avoid trouble is also required at the first planting of rice, and at other stages in the agricultural cycle. Every year community integration and well-being are bolstered by a ceremony, to be described below, involving the partaking of *nasi semangat* by all.

Illness may be caused by other agents. Some diseases such as malaria, which is uncommon at Rusembilan, are considered by villagers to be caused by the cold air of the mountainous areas where the villager plants his rubber trees and often contracts the disease. The disease itself is visualized as a small beetle and cure depends upon driving the beetle from the body of the sufferer. A number of supernatural techniques exist for this. However, it is being discovered by more and more villagers of Rusembilan that aspirin and quinine-containing drugs are most effective in driving off the beetle. The majority of diseases in this area are caused either directly or indirectly by spirits—usually *hantu.* Their cure generally demands negotiation with the spirit, although occasionally force or threats are effective. Along with these negotiations and infusions of *semangat* go any of a large number of specific roots, barks and herbs, either to please or displease the spirits, and many times, commercial pharmaceutical preparations for the same purpose.

Besides ordinary diseases, spirits are capable of causing mental disorders —for which treatment is essentially the same as for any other spirit-caused disease. However, the course of treatment is usually far longer, and the ultimate cure is never certain. In 1956, there were five individuals in Rusembilan whom other villagers considered to be so afflicted. These individuals ranged in degree of derangement from one man continually in a catatonic state to others, who while perfectly able to lead normal lives most of the time, periodically (during the first week of the new moon) lapsed into "fits" involving confused monologues about presumed persecutors. One woman in the village had from infancy been afflicted with *latah,* a relatively common mental disorder in Southeast Asia and other areas, characterized by sudden and brief periods of paroxysm, use of obscene language, and compulsive imitation of the words and actions of others. While this disease is attributed to a supernatural agency, no attempt has been made to seek a cure since the woman was ordinarily able to carry on her normal activities. Her mimetic behavior never ceased to provide amusement for a number of villagers, some even attempting to induce it intentionally.

Basic to the cure of any disease caused by (or potentially caused by) supernatural agency is exorcism or appeasement of the troublesome spirit. This important art is in the hands of a specialist to be found in practically every Malay village—the *bomo*. Because of his power for good, and the possibilities of intentionally misdirecting these powers, the *bomo* must be a man of high moral character. It is common to find him numbered among the *orang baik* of his community. As well as character, a *bomo* requires both special knowledge or skills associated with his profession, and an initial predisposition toward becoming a *bomo*. This latter element is difficult for the villager to objectify: it is often simply a matter of a young man having intimate contact with a father, grandfather, or other close relative who is a *bomo*. Or it may be based on some slight deviation from the normal personality. A child or youth subject to periodic slight fits, or who falls easily into trances when playing *bomo* games with other children, will often be encouraged to develop these tendencies professionally. The acquisition of requisite knowledge and skill is also facilitated by close contact with a practicing *bomo*. This is perhaps the major reason that the profession, like that of steerer of *kolek*, seems to remain in certain families, often skipping a generation. However, it is said that today it is possible to acquire all the necessary knowledge through reading.

When a patient comes, or is brought to the *bomo* for treatment, or when the *bomo* is called to the house of an ailing individual, the first step is diagnosis of the disease. Usually the ailment will not be one that villagers can clearly identify as having natural causes, otherwise they would have successfully treated it with natural, herbal remedies. Thus there is always strong suspicion that the cause is attributable to some displeased or malevolent spirit. Diagnosis is ordinarily accomplished by the *bomo* putting himself into a trance, and inquiring of the spirits the exact cause. Sometimes it is possible at this time, if the disease is being caused by a spirit, to make arrangements with the offending spirit to quit the ailing individual in return for certain specified favors. It is more usual that contact cannot be made directly with the offending spirit at this time, but only with a knowledgeable spirit who is in the habit of supplying the particular *bomo* with information. In this case arrangements will be set up for a subsequent trance, often involving the patient himself, and a confrontation with the spirit causing the disease. Occasionally, the *bomo's* spiritual informer will indicate the matter that is causing displeasure on the part of the offending spirit and a cure can be accomplished without establishing direct contact with the spirit causing the disease. Such a case occurred in Rusembilan. Here the *bomo* was called in to treat a young woman suffering from constipation. The *bomo* learned from his informant that during a recent pregnancy of the young woman's mother, her father had driven a monitor lizard into a hole in the trunk of a tree, and had blocked the lizard's escape by placing a large rock in front of the hole. As soon as the rock was removed, the young woman recovered (Fraser 1960:173).

The trance involved in the actual cure of a patient with a spiritually caused disease involves elaborate preparations, such as are characteristic of the *peterana* discussed below, including fragrant water, incense, and if this is an important cure, a band of musicians as well. The trance itself, unlike that involved in diagnosis, is formalized. Eight particular spirits must be summoned before any curing trance can be effective. These include a powerful couple, vaguely described as being the first human ancestors descended from Satan's youngest and middle brothers [Setan-su and Setan-ngah (cf. Table 3)], and the four guardian angels of each individual, Michael, Gabriel, Israfil, and Izreal. Other spirits, depending on the particular case, may be invoked by the *bomo*. These are often spirits of the patient's own ancestors, who are presumed (not always correctly) to be well-disposed toward the patient, and who thus may be counted on for whatever further intercession may be required. The *bomo's* spiritual informant is not ordinarily used at this point.

Often, during the trance, the *bomo* will enter into violent, frequently acrimonious debate and bargaining with the offending spirit. Sometimes the spirit chooses the mouth of the patient to speak through, sometimes the *bomo's* mouth. Largely on the basis of these debates and the reports of listening relatives, the reputation of a *bomo* is formed. Of course the curves he attempts must have a fair degree of success, but his ability to strike a hard bargain with an aggressive and unpleasant spirit is most important in building confidence in his powers. At this stage of events, the course of the cure can take one of two directions. Either through debate and negotiation, the spirit can agree to cease molesting the patient in return for some favor, such as periodic offerings or the performance of a spiritual amusement, or the *bomo* can risk taking matters entirely into his own hands and exorcise the spirit.

Exorcism varies in specific details according to the routine found most effective by different *bomo*. Among the elements essential to a cure is incense, which may simply be used for background effect or it may play a positive part in the proceedings, being exhaled by the *bomo* into the mouth and eyes of the patient or rubbed symbolically over his body. Scented water is another necessary ingredient; to this may be added ash from a ritual fire or a number of barks and herbs. The chewing of areca nut, betel leaf, and lime figures prominently in exorcism as it does in most other Malay ritual, ceremonial, and even social occasions. However, the most indispensible element in this ritual is incantation. Often incantations are taken from the Koran, or they may derive from locally syncretized works of Islamic mysticism, or, more frequently they will be traditional spells with or without minor Islamic accretions. A final necessary element in exorcism is *nasi semangat*. The purpose of this varies, again depending on the particular theory of different *bomo*. It is either to provide the patient with an additional amount of spiritual energy to hasten his recovery, or it is used as a bribe to lure the spirit away from the patient. In this latter interpretation, and also sometimes in the former, a part of the *nasi semangat* is taken after the ceremony to a relatively deserted spot outside of the village and left for the spirit.

Certain ailments caused by spirits are of too routine a nature to require the attention of the *bomo*. These are related to the spiritual dangers attendant on childbirth and, unless something goes wrong, are handled as matter of course by the *bidan* or midwife. The most dangerous pregnancy is a woman's first, and a special precautionary ceremony is performed by the *bidan* at this time. During the seventh month of pregancy the midwife comes to "place the child properly." This consists of feeding the mother *nasi semangat* to strengthen her in general, and an abdominal massage to align the embryo correctly. Finally a green coconut is opened over the expectant mother's abdomen and its milk is allowed to run over her. It is considered that subsequent pregnancies will not cause the woman to be as susceptible to spirit-caused ailments as her first, so that repetition of this ceremony is not necessary. Often, directly after childbirth the spirit *Hantu Niyam* enters the womb and begins making loud noises and violent actions. Not only does this cause the woman considerable discomfort but it may cause harm to the new child. This is a situation which the *bidan* cannot handle herself, so that a *bomo* must be summoned immediately. Exorcism of this spirit is relatively simple as long as the summoning of a competent *bomo* has not been delayed too long. For forty days after birth, both the child and its mother are considered to be in a period of great danger. The mother is kept in seclusion and attended only by female relatives and the *bidan* (except for serious complications which must be handled by the *bomo*). After it is ascertained that the child will live, a cord is tied around his waist to protect him from spirits and worms. This cord may be removed after the first forty days of life. Another cord is tied over one shoulder and under the opposite arm of the child at the same time. This is so that the child will "remember his great-grandfather," the spirit of whom will then respond by protecting his descendant from harmful spirits and other agents of disease. This string must never be cut; it will eventually wear away after two or three years.

Mention has already been made of the fact that offending spirits often demand certain favors as the condition of their allowing a cure. A favorite one, which is also highly popular with many villagers, is the *peterana*. This is a public seance staged by the *bomo*, in which the spirits entertain themselves (and the audience) by enacting traditional roles through the medium of the *bomo*, and often the former patient, as contracted by *bomo* and spirit during the cure. The entertainment, held at night, is scheduled to coincide with a period in which there is no fishing. Depending on the seriousness of the illness cured, and to a certain extent on the former patient's financial resources, the performance will run an odd number of nights up to a maximum of seven. The most common length is three nights. If it is reasonably certain that the weather will be fine it is preferable to hold the *peterana* out of doors under a large canopy made from *kolek* sails, otherwise it can be held in either the former patient's or the *bomo's* house, whichever is larger. Before the performance begins, villagers, particularly women and children, start arriving and establishing themselves with a good view of the performing area. The following account of a *peterana* at Rusembilan is taken from the 1956 study (Fraser 1960: 182–84):

> The music is started perhaps a half an hour before the *bomo* begins the main performance. The orchestra consists of a three-stringed violin, two double-ended drums, a two-toned hanging gong, and a large enameled tray which is beaten with chopsticks. On all these instruments, on the

posts of the house, and on the decorations for the performance, small candles are affixed which are allowed to burn themselves out. Food, rice flour, and flower blossoms are brought in, and the *bomo* fans incense over them as well as his own body.

When preparations have been completed, the [former] patient is led onto the stage and seated facing the "father" of the *peterana*. At Rusembilan, the "father" is the violinist and not the *bomo*. The father, to a large extent, directs the course of the *peterana*, asking questions of the spirits and influencing the tenor of the conversations and actions by the tempo of his music. The *bomo* places the food and incense in front of the patient, who is to be the medium during the first part of the performance, and brushes him with water containing the rice flour and blossoms. The music then begins, slowly at first, but with increasing tempo as the patient goes into a trance. During the early stages of the performance, . . . the patient, in a sitting position, will do nothing more during his trances than twitch the muscles of his arms, legs, and back, jerk his body, and sway from side to side. Each trance lasts for about ten or fifteen minutes, during which time the "father" speaks to whatever spirit wishes to converse through the medium. . . . The conversations, in keeping with the purpose of the performance as amusement, are generally of a humorous and occasionally obscene nature and are accompanied by laughter and unsubdued talking among the audience.

Later in the first night's performance and/or on succeeding nights, the spirits become more active in the trances of the medium, and through him they dance and act out whatever "play" is in their mind. Ordinarily, the *bomo* at Rusembilan joins in these "plays," so that two spirits may be acting together. . . . The stage for the *peterana* is always decorated . . . with a white awning spread overhead and hanging with flowers, bananas, and palm-leaf crosses. After the spirits have made known by their conversations that they are ready to start acting, the medium is given a new sarong and a new turban in which he is dressed by the *bomo*. . . . This stage of the performance goes on for as long as the spirits desire to play, sometimes lasting until ten in the morning.[1]

At the conclusion of the *peterana*, offerings of food are left for the spirits in a secluded spot in or near the village. It is after these entertainments that children frequently mimic the actions they have seen, and occasionally fall into trances themselves. These are discouraged by parents. However, even though adults usually deny it, such trance-prone children may be encouraged to consider becoming *bomo* themselves.

Other forms of entertainment for the spirits have ceased being practiced at Rusembilan, although one was still performed in the village as late as 1960, and all continue to some extent in more remote villages. The most important of these is the *silat*. In this performance, two men who have studied both traditional Malay boxing and dancing stage a combination dance and fight for the amusement of the spirits. New sarongs, as in the *peterana*, are usually provided. The first four or five acts of the *silat* consist of stylized sparring, characterized by graceful positioning of hands, feet and body, and occasionally humorous atti-

---

[1] © 1960 by Cornell University. Used by permission of Cornell University Press.

tudes. During the final act each participant, still using traditional movements, attempts to overthrow the other. As late as 1960, the *silat* continued to be one of the more popular forms of entertainment: it took far less time and expense than a full-fledged *peterana*, usually no more than two hours in the late afternoon and evening, and it could be performed easily on short notice. However, sometime after the last performance in 1960, a Thai boxing instructor visited Rusembilan offering to give instruction in his art. Thai boxing is different from Malay boxing in that it is not primarily performed in ritual contexts and no punches or kicks are barred in defeating one's opponent. Several villagers of Rusembilan, skilled at *silat*, challenged the Thai instructor to a fight, feeling that they would be assisted by the spirits. They were all quickly and roundly defeated, and the *silat* has not been performed in the village since.

Wayong kulit, the traditional Malay shadow play depicting scenes from the Ramayana, was in the past used at Rusembilan to entertain the spirits. This has long since been given up in the village, as Chinese entertainers in Pattani regularly put on *wayong kulit* shows with a degree of skill not possible in most villages. Villagers (and presumably the spirits also) find them more entertaining than anything of the sort that could be produced at home. Likewise, the *dike ulu*, a competitive singing contest in which two sides vie with each other in composing humorous and derogatory songs, has died out in Rusembilan and is rapidly dying out in other villages. Villagers still enjoy listening to *dike ulu*, but are now able to do so conveniently by turning on their radios to the Pattani radio station between 10:00 and 12:00 Saturday mornings.

Spirits, aside from causing illness and trouble, also have positive uses in Rusembilan and other Malay villages. It is important to take care of the appropriate spirits if one wishes a particular venture to be successful. In growing rice, particularly at the time of transplantation, suitable offerings have to be made to the spirits of the rice plant. In Rusembilan, many cultivators observe this simply by placing a bowl of colored rice out for the spirits at the time of transplantation, in the belief that the guardian spirit of the village will see that nothing amiss happens during other stages of the agricultural cycle. Other people, especially in inland rice-growing areas, present more elaborate and frequent offerings at each stage of the growing cycle. At the beginning of the fishing season each *kolek* crew holds a small feast to remember the spirits of the sea (who are not only important in their own right, but also have control of the spirits of the individual species of fish). Part of these feasts are offered to the sea spirits so that they may ward off illness and prevent fish from escaping the fishermen's nets. Also before going to sea each dark period of the moon, a *kolek* is symbolically washed with lime juice and scented water and decorated with a few flowers and strips of cloth. Formerly a village-wide ceremony was held in Rusembilan at which major offerings were given the sea spirits. While such ceremonies are still held in a few other fishing villages, they are rapidly dying out. Mention has already been made of the small offering and decoration of the housepost when a new house is being raised. Except for the annual ceremony held for the village guardian spirit, there are no other fixed occasions at Rusembilan for taking care of spirits. A man, if he feels particularly insecure about any undertaking, however, may make small offerings to the appropriate spirits to ensure the success of his venture.

In the past, and possibly today, a small number of men in Rusembilan kept *pelesit*, familiars. These spirits either afforded protection to their owner's house and property or assured him success in fishing. However, there were disadvantages involved in keeping familiars: they had to be given special offerings daily and once a year provided with forty eggs. A *pelesit* may desert its owner when he begins losing his strength. Several successful and wealthy fishermen are recalled at Rusembilan, who, on losing their *pelesit*, quickly lost their fortunes. If the familiar decides to remain with its owner, it is then the responsibility, on the death of the owner, for his children to care for the spirit lest illness or harm befall someone else in the community. In this case the diagnosing *bomo* can either demand proper treatment of the spirit by those responsible, or can perform an expensive ceremony to send the spirit permanently away.

Villagers know of various forms of magic for calling upon spiritual help, but assert that none of them is of particular importance today. Perhaps the most common types have been love potions on the one hand, and spells and decoctions designed to maintain or re-establish marital fidelity. Magic concerned with strength in battle and invulnerability is also spoken of frequently as important. Stories are told of the effectiveness of a particular form of this used in the Malayan crisis of the 'fifties. Malays engaged in fighting in the jungle would write passages from the Koran on scraps of paper, dropping them in the trail behind them. The pursuing enemy coming upon such a charm would suddenly find himself beset by all manner of insects, diseases, and general misfortune. The cure for magically caused afflictions is essentially the same as that for any other ailment, with the difference that, when the sorcerer is identified, the *bomo* attempts to persuade him to give up his practice. This persuasion is generally effective as persistent practitioners of magic are treated harshly by the community, even killed.

Fasts, Feasts, and the Imam

No hard and fast line can be drawn between the traditional, shamanistic elements of Malay culture and those elements which are Islamic. As has already been seen, even the shamanistic curing seances often draw heavily on Islam for their most central ingredients, the exorcistic incantations. Likewise, all but the most strictly Islamic occasions (those limited to community religious personnel and teachers in Koranic schools) involve at least a certain amount of traditional belief.

While all events occur according to the will of Allah, and the attempt to foretell them is, strictly speaking, prohibited, divination and the reading of omens is often an essential element in the planning of any important undertaking. The selection of marriage partners, one of the most crucial undertakings in an individual's or family's life, almost universally involves some sort of divination to ensure against gross mismatching. Professional diviners may be called in to present an accurate and detailed picture of the anticipated marriage. However, usually the villagers are content to rely on persons of less professional skill, numerous in any village, for a general idea of the prospects. Divination of this sort by either professionals or amateurs relies on a cabalistic alphabet which is found in one of the two or three "sacred" books which along with the Koran is found in the possession of every village Imam and other religious leader. The method is relatively smple: numerical values are assigned from the book to each letter in the name of both prospective bride and groom; these are added together, divided by nine (in some cases a different divisor), and the remainder can be "read" to indicate the future of the particular match. Within this book are also lists of auspicious and inauspicious days, dates which will react either favorably or unfavorably with given individuals, and a number of signs of good or of ill which must be looked for before starting important ventures. In addition to such omens, there are also a number of traditional Malay omens which can influence the success of an undertaking. The day of the week on which one's umbilical cord was cut is likely to be a bad day on which to start anything. Likewise, if one's path is crossed by a snake or a monitor lizard it is well to postpone plans. However, certain birds portend success, as does the fact of one's right nostril being "stronger" than the left.

Failure to see an omen that was present or unfamiliarity with the meaning of an omen vitiates its effectiveness. However, there is a fine line between lack of recognition of the omen and ignoring the significance of a recognized omen. The latter is sure to bring misfortune. The Imam of Rusembilan has been strongly criticized for setting out to buy a motor boat on a day when several omens spelled failure. While the Imam denies being aware of these signs, his father-in-law, also a respected haji, asserts that he had no business not being aware of them. In any event, as will be indicated in Chapter 7, misfortune did befall this particular venture.

Religious leaders in Rusembilan take a firm stand against any belief or practice which is not in accord with a strict interpretation of Islam. However, as seen above, there are occasions when one must be guided in his actions by practical reality. Even religious leaders occasionally become ill and are left with no alternative but to seek the services of a *bomo*. Furthermore, if a spirit requests that a religious leader be present at a *peterana*, even though this man may object to such performances on religious grounds, he will be present, as he understands the danger involved in not heeding the request of a spirit. There is a haji, a highly respected religious teacher, living in a village not far from Rusembilan who has discovered that he possesses great powers for dealing with spirits. Thus, in spite of his religious convictions to the contrary, he has become a well-known and successful *bomo* with little harm to his reputation as a religious leader and teacher.

Once a year at Rusembilan, and many other villages, a ceremony takes place during which the Imam and the *bomo* actively cooperate for the well-being of the community. This is the ceremony held to honor and propitiate the village guardian spirit (who happens also to be the spiritual protector against cholera). In addition to making offerings of meat, eggs, and glutenous rice to the spirit, the *bomo* supervises the preparation of sufficient *nasi semangat* for the entire community, and participates in the recitation of prayers led by the Imam. Usually the *bomo*, along with the community's religious leaders, delivers a special prayer himself. During this prayer, the *bomo* "remembers" the past great men of the village—who, of course, by now are spirits. As mentioned, the religious leaders of the village give individual prayers seeking continued well-being for the village. *Nasi semangat* is then served for everyone in the community to eat. Finally the Imam leads the assembled men (women and children are excluded as in formal religious services) in the *sembayang hajat*, or afternoon prayers. The religious leaders of the community explain that, although they are opposed to the propitiation of spirits, this ceremony is directed at keeping the village free of evil, sickness, and ghosts and involves prayers to Allah. It is therefore necessary that they participate in this religious function.

While the religious leaders may feel some conflict or at least some discomfort in the juxtaposition of Islam and traditional spiritual beliefs, the ordinary Malay villager has no difficulty in reconciling these two historically different traditions. He believes in spirits and their control because they are part of his reality and he has seen them controlled. He is also a devout Muslim. He is punctilious in saying his five daily prayers (although the last two are often omitted by fishermen at sea) and often adds two additional prayers out of a desire for virtue rather than religious necessity. He will not eat pork, nor take alcoholic drink, and considers contact with a wet dog defiling. It is rare that the requisite forty men do not show up at the village mosque in Rusembilan on Friday—thus formal religious services are held almost every week. These people are extremely conscientious in their observation of Ramadan, the fasting month, although spending the day without food or drink is often hard on fishermen who must perform vigorously throughout much of the night. There is little or no attempt to evade full payment of the *zakat,* or annual religious tithe, nor are alms denied the beggars who are always to be found in and around the municipal market in Pattani. The pilgrimage to Mecca, while considered virtuous rather than religiously necessary, is sought by as many as can afford the 12,000 mile round trip. The fact that there were ten hajis in Rusembilan in 1964 is indicative of its importance.

In spite of his sincere devotion to Islam, the Malay villager feels free to reinterpret its demands to fit conditions of his Southeast Asian culture. A major area of reinterpretation is in the treatment of women. As has already been seen, it is the wives of the fishermen of Rusembilan who tend to be dominant in economic matters. The only time a Malay woman sees a veil is during a formal wedding ceremony, and it is now becoming common for a bride to substitute sun glasses for the veil. Only in matters dealing with formal religion and the mosque is there segregation of adult women from men. No woman may hold office in the religious organization, and during services in the mosque, which are not compulsory for women, they are seated in a separate section screened off from the men. Separation of the sexes also occurs at most *makan pulot* which probably relates both to the religious nature of many of these feasts, and to the traditional division of labor which keeps the women busy preparing and serving the food while the men eat. The seclusion of postpubescent girls until marriage has already been mentioned, which, while in accord with Islamic doctrine, also serves the important function of providing the girl with intensive instruction in domestic arts.

Prohibition of gainful occupation on the Sabbath is another area which has had to bow to local necessity. Until very recently, Rusembilan was one of the few fishing villages in South Thailand from which fishermen did not go to sea Thursday night. The Imam held the very strong opinion that religion demanded the cessation of economic activities from sundown Thursday until sundown Friday. Although the fishermen of Rusembilan acceded to the Imam's demands, they were not happy to see the boats of other villages going out seven nights a week, bringing in revenue on Friday as on any other morning. Finally, at about the same time that the government changed from Friday to Sunday as the legal holiday in South Thailand, the men of Rusembilan started, over the protests of the Imam, to fish Thursday night. In like manner, many of the hajis of Rusembilan who are supposed to be entirely supported by the *zakat* contributions of the villagers and by fees for religious instruction, ignore this ideal and indulge in ordinary economic activities. Most do not engage in either fishing or the manual labor of cultivation (two or three do plow and plant their own fields, and one has only recently retired from steering a *kolek*) but many act the role of entrepreneur, owning fishing boats, coconut plantations, or rice fields which may be worked for them by others.

The day-to-day obligations of the villager as a Muslim are simply routine matters for him. However, being a Muslim is not all routine. There is an annual round of ceremonies and festive occasions which the people look forward to with eager anticipation. These are in addition to the periodic shamanistic rituals and the celebrations in connection with the individual's life cycle. The most important event in the Islamic calendar is the month of fasting, Ramadan. Two days before the beginning of the month most families in Rusembilan prepare numerous banana-leaf packets of glutenous rice which they distribute widely to all their friends, relatives, and neighbors. Once the beginning of the month is announced (the precise beginning is determined by sighting the new moon), nothing may be taken into the body during the hours from sunup to sundown. This includes not only food and drink, but also tobacco smoke (these villagers are avid cigarette smokers), saliva (there is considerable spitting throughout the month) and injections. Every evening at sunset, after the afternoon prayers have been said, the drum at the mosque is beaten loudly giving notice that the food and drink already prepared by the women of the village may be taken. As the month wears on, particularly after the entire Koran has been read through by those attending reading sessions with the Imam every evening of the month, these fast-breaking meals become large, gay parties. Some are held in the mosque, some in the coffee shops, and some in the homes of individuals. The fast-breaking, whether as a private meal or in the form of a large feast, begins with sweets and a sweet drink, followed by large quantities of rice and meat curry with assorted side dishes of vegetables, fish and other delicacies, and finally distribution of cigarettes. Daily activities during Ramadan are somewhat altered. People prefer to sleep as much of the day as they can. Whatever strenuous physical activity can be put off is. However, fishing must go on, often meaning that the fishermen miss the fast-breaking meal on shore and must break their own fast together at sea. On the twenty-seventh day of Ramadan, the single *zakat* levied in Rusembilan is collected, the immediate purpose of its collection at this point being to provide the poor with plenty at the time of the final fast-breaking festivities on the first of the next month.

Hari Raya Puasa [great day (after) fasting] marks the beginning of the month following Ramadan and an end to daily fasting for all but a few who will continue the fast for another six days either to display religious virtue or because it has been necessary for them to break the main fast. On *Hari Raya,* however, no one may fast. This is a gala occasion when all dress in their finest and newest clothing (usually purchased especially for the occasion). There is much visiting back and forth throughout the village and great quantities of food are available for friends. A special service is conducted in the mosque during the morning, invariably drawing greater numbers that at any other time of the year. In the afternoon, many of the villagers set off gaily for Pattani where the opening of an annual carnival is timed to coincide with this day. Here they watch Malay dancing, Thai boxing, and bullfighting, and enjoy the rides and numerous entertainment booths. In the evening three- or four-foot torches of coconut shells are lighted. Firecrackers made either from gunpowder or bamboo sections filled with water are sealed and heated until they explode.

Another *Hari Raya* is marked at the conclusion of the six optional days of fasting. This is never celebrated with the gusto of *Hari Raya Puasa,* and, indeed, may not be celebrated at all. A third feast day, *Hari Raya Haji* (great day of the pilgrim) is celebrated almost as elaborately as *Hari Raya Puasa* if a villager is planning to make the pilgrimage to Mecca that year, or if one is returning. The shipping companies that provide transport to and from Mecca attempt to time their return so that the new hajis will arrive home just before this day. Other days in the ceremonial calendar are less festive and more concerned with intensification of religious devotion. Chief among these are *Ashura,* corresponding to the Day of Atonement and *Maulud,* celebrating the birth of the Prophet. *Maulud* is an occasion for numerous feasts in the villages. The first is always held in the mosque (or *balaisa,* see below) where important religious guests, religious students, or the Imam read from the life of the Prophet. Villagers wanting to honor the Prophet, particularly those wanting to mark the completion of their children's first study of the Koran, will hold subsequent feasts for the honored guests and religious leaders. So many villagers in Rusembilan desired to hold *Maulud* feasts in 1964 that the celebration extended over three days.

Throughout the preceding pages the chief religious structure of Rusembilan has been referred to as a mosque. In strict fact this is not so, for a mosque must be of permanent construction such as stone or concrete, and it must contain a formal lectern or pulpit from which services are conducted. The wooden structure in Rusembilan is correctly a *surau* rather than a *masjid,* or mosque. It does function within the community as a true mosque, being the center of congregation for the worshippers and being the site of the drum which calls villagers to prayer and announces other important occasions. In addition to the *surau* of Rusembilan which is located in one of the hamlets away from the beach, there is also a *balaisa*, an even less formal religious congregation center, in the main village immediately adjacent to the Imam's house. Because of its convenience for the Imam and the majority of villagers, it is in the *balaisa* that most of the important religious feasts take place, and here that the village children receive instruction in memorizing the Koran. Both the *surau* and the *balaisa* are cared for by a mosque committee made up of the three religious officials and nine lay members selected by them from among the more formally religious members of the community. As well as physical maintenance of the two structures, the committee has the responsibility of making arrangements for important celebrations and feasts to be held. It is this committee, also, which organizes the village work parties necessary for building the structures in the first place, for major repairs, and for such projects as moving the *balaisa* bodily when the Imam built a new house for himself and his family. The three formally appointed religious officials, the Imam, the *khatib,* and the *bilal* (muezzin) are selected from a list of nominations submitted by the villagers to the provincial *Majalis Ugama* [(Islamic) Religious Board]. Once the selection has been made, it is the district officer in the government hierarchy who, following a regular Friday service in the mosque, actually invests these men with office.

Each Thai province with significant Muslim population has its *Majalis Ugama* to look after the welfare of adherents to Islam. It meets monthly with the provincial governor to review administrative and legal matters which relate to religion. It has on occasion been instrumental in achieving or restoring what Muslims of Thailand have considered their religious rights, such as the presence in court of a *kadi,* or religious advisor, as well as the Thai judge. In addition the *Majalis* keeps records of the number of mosques and religious officials in the province, serves to collect and redistribute village *zakat* funds, and provides advice to litigants both official and unofficial in religious disputes or civil disputes involving religion. It is also charged with the responsibility of approving construction plans for proposed mosques, and, in this role, has come in for some adverse criticism in recent years. The Thai government, in part as a gesture of good intention to the Malay population of the South, and in part to emphasize its policy of recognizing no difference in its citizens except religion, decided to build a large mosque on the outskirts of Pattani town. The structure, which cost the government 4 million *baht* ($200,000), is indeed impressive, and is visible to all who travel the main highway between Pattani and Yala. However, in deciding on its construction in the first place, and its site in the second, the government, and by implication the *Majalis Ugama* of Pattani, neglected to account for the fact that within half a mile of the new structure is the traditional main mosque of Pattani, revered by the people and once used by the rajas of Pattani. They further neglected to consider that many of the Malays of the town and province would see this gesture as completely a political move, devoid of the type of spirit which was purported to motivate it.

It has been implied already that there is a certain amount of conflict between religious leaders of a community and the traditional, economically oriented leaders. The religious leaders are certainly respected throughout the community and are "good men." The traditional leaders are also good Muslims. However, the religious leaders are not properly considered *orang baik* in terms of secular community leadership. Along with less prestigeful religiously minded people, such as lay members of the mosque committee, they form a group providing leadership in religious affairs and in matters pertaining to marriage, divorce, and certain types of property settlement. No one would think of consulting them on problems of an economic nature. This separation, or conflict, is the result of certain conflicts in the basic values instilled into every individual growing up in these Malay villages. It is significant that the community in a sense recognizes this latent conflict and has established periodic activities, such as the ceremony to the village guardian spirit, designed to subordinate these conflicting areas of authority to a larger welfare and integration of the entire village. Likewise, in practically every ceremony connected with the life cycle of an individual, there is a blending of the strictly Islamic with the traditional Malay. These dual elements, stressed at a time of general value intensification and reaffirmation, again help to ensure harmony and integration within the individual members of the community, and, indeed, may even permit some individuals to function effectively, as the haji who became a successful *bomo*, in both apparently contradictory spheres at once.

Religion and the Crises of Life

Every individual in every culture must pass through a number of more or less distinct transition points in the course of growing from infancy to old age. Each of these points, representing the embarkation into a new stage of life, is always characterized by a certain amount of tension and stress either for the individual himself or for his family group. Some of these transitions are biologically determined, such as birth itself, attainment of physiological maturity, and death. However, every society recognizes certain transitions which are culturally determined, or at least where the overlying cultural interpretation is of more importance than the physiological fact. Recognition of an individual as a social or religious person or both, attainment of adult status in the society with attendant responsibilities, and marriage represent some of the more important and universal of these culturally determined transitions.

The chief transitional points in the life cycles of individuals of Rusembilan will be described briefly in the paragraphs that follow. The main emphasis will be placed on the integrating and intensifying function of religion at these times. In particular, it will be pointed out how in almost every case there is a combination either into one set of rituals, or separately in a necessary ritual series, of the two systems of values and beliefs found in these villages.

Birth represents a tremendously important transition for the family into which the new member of society is being born, particularly if it is the first child. It may be a time of considerable anxiety and stress. The protective attention given the expectant mother during pregnancy by the midwife and the administration of *nasi semangat* has already been described. Although the midwife is in attendance during labor, and the *bomo* on call if necessary, no special precautions are taken at this time. Once delivery is completed, the afterbirth is taken by the midwife or a female member of the family, washed, and wrapped with salt in a clean cloth. It is either kept in the house during the mother's forty-day seclusion, after which time it is buried, or it is buried immediately, usually under the house, but at any rate in a clean sandy spot where it will not be molested by children or spirits who might harm the new child. The midwife cuts off half of the newborn's umbilical cord with a bamboo knife used only for this purpose, allowing the other half to drop off of its own accord sometime later. The day of the week on which this latter half drops off will be an inauspicious day for the rest of the life of the individual, while the day of the week on which he was born will be auspicious. As soon after birth as the mother can receive company, intimate female friends and relatives visit her, bringing with them gifts of bananas and money. For a first child both the number of visitors and the amount of the individual gifts are greater. Throughout labor and delivery, the father and all other men (unless the *bomo* is required) are kept out of the house, nor is the mother allowed male visitors (including her husband) for the forty days following the birth of the child. The only exception to this rule occurs soon after the child is born when the father along with a few religious leaders are allowed in to whisper a prayer to Allah into the child's ear, the right if it is a boy, the left if it is a girl. As mentioned above, the child soon after birth is provided with two strings to protect it from harmful spirits and illness and to commit it to the protection of its "grandfather." Thus the child, as soon as possible, is assured supernatural protection covering the gamut from Allah to ancestral spirits. The mother continues to be in spiritual danger for the forty days during which she is kept secluded, ministered to by females only, and "roasted" by a small fire kept burning next to her for the purpose of keeping off evil spirits. In addition, certain types of foods considered "cold" (for example, most vegetable foods) are prohibited to her and her husband. During pregnancy she was not allowed to eat "hot" foods, such as meat and some fruits.

When the child is about three months old (in theory it should be seven days old) a small ceremony is held to give formal recognition of the child's membership as an individual within the community. This is the *akikah*, or naming ceremony whereby the child is formally recognized by the religious organization of the village. A name, which has previously been chosen by the parents from the roster of Muslim saints, is repeated several times into the ear of the child by the Imam or occasionally a highly respected relative of the child. After the name has been "implanted" on the child, its mouth is ceremonially "opened." This consists of passing first a silver, then a gold ring dipped in salt water over the child's lips several times. Then the original namer places a small amount of cooked rice in the child's mouth and repeats the name, which is reiterated by all the relatives and religious leaders in attendance. All rise and sing of the character of Mohammed, "so that the child may grow up to be like him," and each guest in turn cuts a small lock of hair from the child's head. This completes the child's part in the ceremony. He is now placed in a decorated cradle in the middle of the room while the guests are seated for a meal of mutton curry and rice—women and unbelievers are not allowed to partake.

The child has now been formally recognized by both community and Islam. During the relatively carefree years before his assumption of adulthood he is, however, making preparations for his future status. This is the period during which he begins his religious instruction, which will be dealt with more fully in the following chapter. Two important events mark his progress in this area. The completion of his study of the Koran in the village is one, and is expected of all children, both male and female. The other, only for very serious students of religion, marking the conclusion of their formal study, is the pilgrimage to Mecca. As mentioned previously, a small celebration is usually held to mark the first of these events in a child's religious growth; if possible, it is held at the time of the celebrations of the birthday of Mohammed. This confers on the child, in theory, full membership in the Muslim community.

The most significant transition in a person's life is that from childhood to full adult status. This transition is seen as a more or less drawn-out period rather than a single point of transition. For males it is marked most significantly at the beginning, for females at the end. The ceremony marking male puberty (although the ceremony need not correspond with the physiological fact) is perhaps the most elaborate held at Rusembilan. In this, as in the marriage ceremony marking the end of the transition period, traditional and Islamic elements play an approximately equal part. While this ceremony involves the universal Islamic custom of circumcision, its non-Islamic aspects are equally important, as indeed, its name implies: *Masuk Jawi* (entering Malay-hood). The ceremony involves two feasts, the first primarily for the Imam, religious leaders of the village, and respected hajis and religious teachers from surrounding villages. During this feast passages are read from the Koran and prayers are offered for the well-being of the boy in his new adult status. The second feast, a traditional *makan pulot* is usually the largest *makan pulot* a village family ever holds. Everyone from the boy's village, his relatives, their friends and connections from many surrounding villages attend, each bringing gifts of money—the closer the relationship the larger the gift.

The ritual leading up to the circumcision usually occurs the day following the large *makan pulot*. It commences with a parade through the village in which the boy, resplendently dressed and decorated, is borne on an elephant, horse, or the shoulders of his relatives for all to see. He is taken after the parade to a decorated chair, corresponding to the chair used in the marriage ceremony, where he is fed *nasi semangat* by a close friend or relative of his father (or a man of great respect) who has been chosen as his ceremonial sponsor. This sponsor, like the one acquired by the girls on their marriage, functions much as a godparent to the young adult. There are no formal obligations involved in this relationship, but ties of mutual affection and helpfulness similar to those of close kinship are implied. After spiritual reinforcement with *nasi semangat*, the boy is led by his sponsor to a room where a specialist is waiting to perform the actual circumcision. The wound must be kept bound until it is entirely healed, during which time the youth may not eat "hot" foods. Although the *Masuk Jawi* is the most important ceremony in a boy's life, there is no rite marking a girl's puberty. She enters seclusion in her home where she will spend the transitional period until her marriage.

Masuk Jawi purports to admit young men into full adult status. However, as pointed out, it more accurately marks the beginning of a gradual transition of which marriage is the final event. The youth, like the young woman, is in a sense serving apprenticeship during this period. Actually, even marriage does not immediately and of itself launch the new couple into the full responsibilities of adult status. This must await the birth of their first child. Like the *Masuk Jawi*, the marriage ceremony consists of two parts, each marked with a feast, one primarily Islamic, the other traditional Malay. The first of these, usually preceding the second by some two to four weeks, consists of the Islamic sanction for the marriage (this is the only ceremony performed in the case of remarriages). Here formalized bargaining takes place over the previously agreed upon amount of the bride price [this varies between 2000 and 4000 *baht* ($100 –$200)]. The bride takes no part in this ceremony, her place being taken in the negotiations by a male relative. In addition to the bargaining and a feast, witnesses must attest to the single status of both parties to the marriage. The ceremony is concluded with recitation of prayers and a short formalized sermon delivered by the Imam of the bride's village.

The second part of the marriage ceremony is the occasion for a *makan pulot*, second only in size and importance to that held in connection with the *Masuk Jawi*. On the day of this ceremony, the girl remains in her house while she is prepared and instructed for the coming events by her ceremonial sponsor. During these preparations her teeth are filed evenly and whatever facial hair she may have is plucked out. Her hair is arranged in an elaborate style and she is dressed in a costume agreed upon by the two families involved. This may be either traditional dress of batiks and blouse and short jacket for the young woman, and white coat with sarong-covered trousers for the young man, or Islamic dress with flowing robes for the male and a full, long dress with veil for the female. After the last of the guests invited only for the *makan pulot* have been served and left, the goom's party begins to approach the bride's house. This party is made up of friends and close young male relatives of the groom. They make their presence known by singing loud praises to the Prophet or by exploding firecrackers (or firearms). The groom is met at the foot of the house ladder by a female relative of the bride and is led into the house and seated on the decorated wedding seat beside his bride. The bride's sponsor then touches both on the forehead with a mixture of betel leaf, areca nut, and lime, and feeds them *nasi semangat*. The sharing by the couple of *nasi semangat* seals the marriage. This is finally followed by the viewing of the bride discussed in Chapter 3. Usually after this ceremony the groom returns to his own village for two or three days before returning to his bride. Consummation of the marriage, always postponed for three days after this, often is not achieved for two or three weeks because of the shyness of the bride and the magnitude of her transition out of seclusion.

Divorce and remarriage are perfectly admissible under Islamic law. However, they are not marked in the traditional sector of the culture. Divorce before consummation of a marriage (which is fairly common) requires only the concurrence of bride and groom, and a return of the "bride price." Although common, such cases would be more common it it were not for the intercession of the Imam. (The Imam of Rusembilan indicates that of ten to fifteen marriages a year in the village, four or five end in divorce.) Unless it is objectively apparent that the marriage will not endure, the Imam tries to persuade the groom to remain with his bride, pointing out both her virtues and the mutual responsibilities of the couple to one another and to the community. After a marriage has been established for a year or more, intercession by the Imam is no longer called for if a couple plans to separate. All that is necessary is for the man to utter to his wife three times before witnesses, "I divorce you." In the case of a woman seeking divorce, she must be able to show sufficient cause for such action to the Imam. The "bride price" is not returned in case of divorce, but the husband is required to divide with his wife all property acquired during the period of marriage.

Remarriage of a woman involves only the first, Islamic ceremony: ceremonial sponsorship, joint eating of *nasi semangat*, and activation of the kinship and ceremonial network in feasting play no part. Polygamy, like divorce and remarriage, does not find formal sanction in traditional Malay belief, although it is permitted under Islamic law. Its practice is practically nonexistent in Malay villages in South Thailand, both because of the expense of supporting more than one woman, and the fact that village women "will not stand for it." Where it exists, it is confined to wealthy hajis and religious leaders.

Adult life in a Malay village is characterized by security. Even the decline into old age and final retirement from economic pursuits is a gradual, almost imperceptible transition. As was indicated in Chapter 3, security is usually provided for an aging couple by their youngest daughter and her husband who gradually assume management of the family house and some of its other real assets. Even lacking this arrangement, an older couple can count on the support of other relatives and friends in the village in case of need.

The moment death occurs in the village, the drums of the mosque (and *balaisa* as well at Rusembilan) notify the whole community of the fact. All activity stops and may not be commenced again until the ritual and interment are completed. Friends and neighbors begin to gather outside of the house in which death occurred. Women visit the house, leaving a small gift of money; men contribute their services in constructing the coffin. As soon as the coffin has been prepared and funeral garments of new white cloth have been fashioned, the Imam arrives to prepare the body for burial. The body, held by a relative, is completely bathed by the Imam, using water specially purified with herbs and clay. It is then rinsed and dried and all orifices plugged with cotton. While the body is being completely swathed in funeral garments by the Imam, the relative who held the body during washing is massaged to restore his strength after contact with the corpse. After purifying himself, the Imam leads a series of prayers for the deceased, upon which a procession of men take the laden coffin to its shallow grave in the village burial ground. Within the household of the deceased, prayers will be said at least seven times a day for the first seven days after death. At this time a small feast is held for religious leaders of the community, marking the conclusion of the first intense mourning period. Another small feast is held at the end of forty days, indicating the end of general mourning. These feasts serve the dual purpose of committing the deceased to the mercy of Allah, and of ensuring that the spirit of the deceased will not cause harm to its living relatives and neighbors. Additional feasts may be given on the anniversary of the death, usually for no more than three years. However, as time elapses, the Islamic function of the anniversary feasts becomes less and less important, while honoring the deceased according to traditional custom becomes more important, at last becoming indistinguishable from "remembering" the spirit of an ancestor.

6

Learning to Live in Rusembilan

Basic Values and Early Training

WE HAVE EXAMINED the major transition points in the life of an individual and the interplay of two differing sets of values within the ceremonial observance of these points. The ways in which a child is taught the basic values of his culture will be considered in this chapter: what these values are and how they give meaning to life and also are made meaningful by the rituals marking the passage from one stage of life to another.

During infancy, the child at Rusembilan is constantly in the company of others. If he is not being held and fondled by his own mother or father, it will be an elder sibling, a relative, friend, or neighbor, who is gently rocking the baby while he pursues some other activity, often talking. During his waking hours, and during many in which he is asleep, an infant is practically never put down. If the infant appears unhappy he is fondled or fed by whomever happens to be holding him. Although any nursing mother may feed the infant, it is more usual for his own mother (who is never far away) to tend to this. There is little or no concern over the infant's wetting or soiling. Usually the child can simply be held away from the person holding him and the excreta covered with beach sand or rinsed through the cracks in the floor boards indoors. Infants, and small children also, are not encumbered with clothing. Girls are frequently provided with a tiny chain-link apron suspended from the waist, "for the sake of decency." Also every child must wear, after it is forty days old, at least one silver bracelet. This is to indicate that the child is not poor.

Weaning and toilet training are both very gradual processes. The child is introduced to rice porridge or oatmeal or both soon after he is forty days old and gradually is given more and more of a normal adult diet. He continues to nurse whenever he wants, and by the time he is two or three has usually given it up of his own accord. With the advent of another child, this process may have to be somewhat accelerated by the mother, but rarely before the nursing child is two. Likewise, toilet training simply consists of suggesting to the child that he relieve himself outside of the house. He soon learns by example what areas are appropriate.

The period of childhood after weaning and learning to talk can be divided into two rough stages. The first of these lasts until the child is around five or six and is characterized by his large measure of dependence on his parents or siblings. During the second stage, lasting until nine or ten years of age, the child has considerable freedom from adults, although he may be given the responsibility of caring for younger siblings. During this period his formal religious and secular education begins. Before six years of age most of the basic values are instilled in the child by precept and example. The formal values which parents hope to instill into their children can be broadly dichotomized as those directed

TABLE 4

BASIC VALUES AS INTERPRETED BY THE IMAM
AND THE BOMO OF RUSEMBILAN

Category	Iman	Bomo
Personal character	To know God To learn to pray To learn the Law (Koranic)	To be good (baik) To be industrious To learn the Koran
Relations with others	Not to sin against the Law Not to quarrel To follow the Imam	Not to cause others trouble Not to quarrel To obey one's parents

at building personal character on the one hand, and those directed at maintaining good relations with one's fellows in the community. There is no universal agreement on what constitute the most important of these values. It is not surprising that the chief difference of opinion falls between the religiously oriented group of villagers following the Imam, and the traditionally oriented group following the *bomo* and many of the *orang baik* of the community. Table 4 summarizes the chief qualities that parents should seek to develop in their children as seen by the Imam of Rusembilan and the *bomo*. There is an underlying similarity in the two lists, although on only two points is there full agreement: that children (and adults) should not quarrel, and that they should know the Koranic Law (*hukim*, law, as such was not mentioned by the *bomo*). Perhaps such full agreement is more apparent than real, for the Imam interdicts quarreling on the basis that hard feelings between individuals are a sin against God, while the *bomo* implicitly fears lest community harmony and mutual helpfulnes be destroyed. The average family in Rusembilan, however, does not draw such a precise dichotomy between these two areas of culture. As parents everywhere, Malay parents "know" how to raise their children and what kind of behavior is appropriate to their own way of life.

One of the most important considerations is the physical safety of the child. Such things as cooking fires, sharply pointed murex shells, and unprotected wells are potentially dangerous and young children are conscientiously kept from them. Children may handle the common large knife, or *parang*, but adults try to see that they do it in manner which will cause them no harm. One of the few things which a child is made to do (usually against his wishes) is bathing. As soon as he is able to, his mother will attempt through persuasion or sometimes physical coercion, to induce him to bathe from head to foot at the nearest well three times a day. Bathing before prayer is an essential part of the religious life of the Muslim villager, and it is considered important that children form this good habit even before it is necessary for them to perform prayers. Also it is important that a child's language is respectful and pious. Mistakes in address and the use of kin terms are dealt with gently and with amusement. The use of such words as "pig" and "dog" however, will bring an immediate and severe scolding or even a pinch on the cheek from any adult present.

Children must be discouraged from annoying others, particularly adults. As a matter of fact, it is rare that they do, as they are usually occupied with another, older child playing on the beach with his own group of friends. If a child is annoying adults by crying for no obvious reason which can be remedied, he is implored to stop or to leave the group of adults. As a last resort, he will be told that if he doesn't stop crying he will be taken in the night by either a *hantu* or the Japanese. This is almost always effective. While standards of modesty are gradually being developed in the child, there is little or no concern with nakedness of children during this first stage of childhood. It is a common sight at Rusembilan to find small children running about the beach with their sarongs draped around their necks in a bundle rather than hanging at their waists. It is only when important visitors from outside the village are present that an attempt is made to keep children properly clad. Such attempts often fail, in which case the offending children are whisked good-naturedly away from the visitors. Quarreling and fighting among children, as among adults, are considered to be wrong, and will be stopped on all occasions. With children, physical separation is frequently employed to expedite the conclusion of the fight. In any case, the child will always be told "Do not quarrel. Play nicely. Be good friends. Be good (*baik*)."

Children are expected to obey the commands of adults and particularly of their own parents. These commands are of two types: those having to do with the development of proper behavior in the child, and those simply for the convenience of the adult. There is little concern if the child ignores the second type; it is laughed off and the adult runs the errand or performs whatever activity he had asked the child to do for him. In matters of the child's own behavior, stricter obedience is expected, and slapping on the side of the head or caning with a rattan stick are occasionally resorted to by more conservative parents. Even so, the Imam of Rusembilan complains that village parents are extremely lax in their disciplinary role. Of course, a balance must be struck. If the parents are too severe, the child will simply leave home, taking refuge usually with grandparents in the village or, if older, even going to another village in which he has relatives. The role of disciplinarian falls mostly on the mother as she is with the child most during early childhood. In some families, however, where the father is present most of the time or where the temperaments of the parents dictate it, the father may assume this role. Even so, it is felt by villagers that a child at this stage belongs to its mother more than to its father. During ceremonial observances, one man will ordinarily appoint himself as unofficial disciplinarian. The job of this man, who must have a loud, fear-inspiring voice, is to keep children from interfering with the performance of the ceremony.

Most of a child's socialization during this stage, however, is based on observing the example of others. The most important models for this are the child's own parents. A girl begins to learn the fundamentals of such domestic activities as cooking and housekeeping. Boys, following their fathers about the village, start learning the appropriate male roles (other then fishing). Also important is the child's exposure to the play gangs of older children, the types of gangs that he himself will be entering later on. As he is often in the charge of an elder sibling, he is included as a matter of course, albeit in a dependent status, in all the activities of the older children, and quickly learns the ways in which his elders maintain harmony within the group.

Throughout childhood, gentle pressure is frequently put on the child to develop cleverness and perseverance. Children are encouraged to attempt new learning as soon as possible. When a child is about ready to talk, many adults will casually spend time with him encouraging him to respond to their own vocalizations. Often this is carried too far, frustrating the child. *Pak Sa's* son Haji Hussain, who had married outside of Rusembilan, was sitting on the beach in front of his father's house one day with his own son about two and one-half years old. Haji Hussain was trying to teach his son to count. While the child could repeat the numbers when his father said them, he was totally unable to put them together in sequence. Hussain persisted in his attempt for about ten minutes during which time several other adults gathered, alternately trying to encourage the child and chiding Haji Hussain for having a "slow" boy. Finally the child was in tears and had to be solaced in the arms of his father. Cleverness is a trait universally desired in children. Many people in Rusembilan today recognize that the cleverness (or wisdom) of the old men is too narrow to meet the needs of life in modern South Thailand, and stress the importance of acquiring the type of knowledge offered by the government schools.

The emphasis on developing cleverness and industry is intensified as a child reaches the age when formal education can begin. Instruction is now largely out of the hands of parents and they direct their efforts toward getting the children to attend school regularly. Some families stress religious education and some stress secular education. Some children may be caned for truancy, while the parents of others seem to have little or no interest in pushing their children into learning. Besides the formal secular and religious education of village children, boys and girls are expected to start assuming the religions obligations which they will have to perform as full members of the religious community as adults. These are largely formal obligations, and often remain so throughout life. In theory, however, once the forms have been learned in childhood, a youth should persist in his religious training to the point where each of the forms bears meaningful relation to the total fabric of his religion. Children of six or seven are expected to begin saying prayers five times each day (presumably the ablutions necessary before prayer are now habitually performed). They learn to treat Friday as a day of prayer and contemplation on which they must not engage in rough activity. However, until a boy has gone through his *Masuk Jawi* ceremony he is not expected to attend the Friday services in the mosque. Children learn during this time to observe the fasting month of Ramadan, and also are expected to make their own *zakat* contribution on the twenty-seventh day of this month.

Perhaps the most important part of a child's life between the ages of six and ten is his membership in one of the groups of children to be found in all Malay fishing villages. Such groups are of less importance in the interior villages as most adult activities are carried out within a short distance of the village—at any rate on dry land. In these villages there is a greater tendency for children of this age to continue the pattern of earlier years, following along and observing their parents as the latter engage in their normal work. In the younger groups, both sexes are represented about equally, as a natural outgrowth of the child's previous dependence on an older sibling who was involved in a play group. Later the groups tend to reformulate along sex lines, as a kind of prelude to the rigid segregation of sexes with the onset of puberty. As each of these groups (numbering ten or fifteen children) develops, a leader emerges. In time, other members of the group not only follow his lead, but also seek his advice on a variety of matters. The leader, like his adult counterpart the *orang baik,* may never be a bully; he executes his leadership through cleverness and wisdom, not through force. There is no "ganging-up on an underdog," and weaker and timider children are urged on all occasions to join in the activities of the group. Younger children in the charge of their older siblings must also be allowed to take part in the group's activities (even though their role is usually a passive one) and the leader tends to see that this is done harmoniously.

Like the boat crew, there is tendency for these childhood groups to maintain continuity over the years. There is some change in the composition of each group, but it is common for a core, usually including the leader, to continue in the same group during the whole period from about six until nine or ten. Other groups are formed continuously as new children become ready to enter them, and these too will continue on with their members until ultimate dissolution. Dissolution is brought about for a number of reasons. Generally the leader of a group will be a brighter-than-average and more industrious individual. Because of this he may well be urged into continuing his formal religious or (more rarely) secular education which will take him away from the village for most of the time. Without a leader the group is apt to fall apart. In addition, other boys are being called on by their parents to take a more active part in the family's economic activities, such as tending cattle, helping in the rice fields, mending nets, or assisting with shoreline fishing operations. Occasionally, a boys' group will persist informally on through adolescence. Usually such adolescent groups spend a considerable amount of time away from the village, sitting in the Malay coffee shops of Pattani, attending the cinema, or traveling to other villages for *makan pulot*. Girls' groups do not persist after the members reach ten or eleven, as this is the time when they are taken into seclusion in their parents homes until marriage three or four years later.

Education: Informal, Formal, and National

Every adult male in Rusembilan is expected to be able to recite the Koran by rote. As a matter of fact, many men and quite a few women can. This recitation is in Arabic, the language of the Koran, so that very few of the villagers understand what they are reciting. In Rusembilan there are only two individuals, the Imam and one other religious leader, who have the slightest understanding of the Arabic they read. In order to accomplish this feat of memorization, every village child must attend a period of instruction twice a day. While it is not essential that girls receive this instruction, almost all of the girls at Rusembilan attend the sessions more or less regularly. This is probably due to the fact that there are number of women there who have been to Mecca, who are respected for their religious knowledge, and who take a fairly active part in the religious life of the community. One of these women is the Imam's wife. In 1956 she was in charge of Koran instruction for the village girls, and, with the involvement of the Imam in the purchase of motor boats, eventually took over the classes for both boys and girls. By 1960, however, because of his wife's pregnancy and the resolution of the motorization problem, the Imam had taken over all classes, a situation more closely in accord with general Malay Muslim practice.

A child usually starts this training at the age of six, although in some cases it is put off until he is seven. At about seven o'clock each morning except Fridays and feast days, the Imam joins the gathered children, reads a short passage from the Koran, and listens to the children recite it in unison. In general the session proceeds in this manner, with children arriving and leaving intermittently. While many children leave sometime between eight and nine o'clock in order to get to the village school, the Imam continues as long as any child is left. As a matter of fact, he encourages children to stay on during the morning hours, and usually a group of five or six boys will be found reciting the Koran until almost noon. Another session is held from four o'clock, when the village school closes, until six. However, as in the morning session, the Imam encourages the children to attend the afternoon session for a longer period. He is ready to begin by two o'clock. The number of years that a child is involved in learning the Koran varies tremendously according to how much time the child devotes to it each day, and how diligently he studies. A hard-working child can master the entire Koran in as little as a year and a half or two, but it is more usual for him to spend from five to seven years at the task.

The Imam of Rusembilan, in common with other Imams, feels that parents in the village are not sufficiently strict with their children in the matter of their attendance in these classes. If a child is absent from more than one or two sessions, the Imam will go and talk severely with the parents. Children who do not pay attention during recitation may be caned by the Imam (in contrast with the village school teacher who may not strike a child). As pointed out above, the Imam often encourages the children to continue their Koran lessons after nine o'clock in the morning, thereby causing them to be late for the beginning of the village school, or to miss it altogether. Several religious leaders in Rusembilan have not allowed their children to attend the village school at all, preferring to have their initial education confined to religious studies to be followed by further religious study at the *pondok*, or religious "secondary" school.

Along with rote memorization of the Koran, the Imam attempts to teach the children a little bit about the meaning of religion. Many village parents give their children no religious instruction, so that the Imam must start with the most rudimentary aspects. Basic to religion is prayer. Not only must the child be taught the proper words (in Arabic) for use during his daily prayers, but he must also learn the proper attitudes, gestures, and postures. After this fundamental has been mastered, the Imam is most interested in teaching the children "the way to know God." This does not imply a personal knowledge, but a very formal, legalistic knowledge gained through knowledge of the Koran and an understanding of the most important of the Koranic laws. Especially apt and diligent students may also be given private or semiprivate instruction by the Imam or another religious leader in the Malay language religious books. These include interpretive works on the Koran as well as works dealing mainly with magical and divinatory topics cast in an Islamic content. Because the Malay language is written in Arabic script, the study of these books in Malay after the student has become familiar with the script itself in the Koran generally awakens the student to the fact that he can read (and write with little extra effort) his own language.

It is expected that every village child will complete this basic course of religious instruction. However, many boys reach the age when they can start their apprenticeship in fishing before learning the Koran, and simply drop out of Imam's classes. When the Imam feels that a child has adequately memorized the Koran and is sufficiently well-grounded in the fundamentals of religion, an informal examination is arranged. This is usually not given by the village Imam, but by a religious teacher or Imam from elsewhere. The examiner will recite a passage from the Koran, and the child will respond by reciting the next passage. This continues until the examiner is satisfied that the child has learned the Book well, if perhaps not letter perfect. The examination is often followed by a small feast for religious leaders to celebrate the child's graduation. He is now ready, if his parents so choose, to pursue more formal studies in the *pondok*.

At the same time that the Malay child begins his religious training from the village Imam, he is also supposed to enter the national educational system. Education in Thailand is both free and compulsory for four years. (Since 1960 the period of compulsory education has been extended to seven years, but this is yet to be implemented in many rural areas.) Education and educational policy is in the hands of the Ministry of Education in Bangkok which sets the standards and determines the curriculum for all of Thailand. The implementation (including matters of finance) of the national educational program, however, is left to a large degree to district and provincial education officers. The sympathetic understanding or impatience of these men toward the special educational problems in the South has a great deal to do with the different rates of educational development in the different districts of Pattani, Yala, and Narathiwat. A basic goal of the system is to have a school available within walking distance by every child. This goal is close to realization in the coastal areas of the South, but far from it in the more sparsely settled interior districts. Provision of a school building, however, does not assure attendance by village children.

While literacy and education in general are stated values of the majority of adults in Rusembilan, there are certain factors which make the education offered in the village school less than satisfactory. A basic factor, common throughout Thailand, is the inadequacy of training of some of the rural teachers. The minimum educational requirements for teachers are two years of teacher training after a ten-year course of general education. However, many of the rural teachers in Thailand have had little, if any, more education than the first four primary grades which they are expected to teach in village schools. Language presents an even greater problem in the South. The language of instruction in Thai government schools is, of course, Thai. The language spoken by the Malay village children is Malay. It is both amusing and disheartening to walk into the school at Rusembilan and observe the teacher standing in front of the class with charts and chalkboard, teaching from the government syllabus in Thai, while the children squirm on the benches and chatter among themselves in Malay.

The head teacher at the Rusembilan school up until July 1964 was considered so incompetent by the villagers that they initiated action to have him removed. Not only did this teacher lecture at his classes in Thai, but he was totally incapable of maintaining any semblance of discipline in the classroom. Attendance was generally only about 15 to 20 percent of enrolled pupils, and the teacher himself was invariably late in arriving and early in leaving—often he failed to show up at all. Although this teacher was the nephew of an important provincial official, both his manifest incompetence and the pressure brought by the villagers through their *naiban* and *kamnan* were sufficient to have him removed. His assistant was also transferred, and three new teachers were given charge of the 182 pupils registered in the four primary grades. The new head teacher was a felicitous choice. Not only was he a Malay Muslim himself, but he was well known and respected by a number of Rusembilan villagers. His first action on appointment was to call on the Imam of Rusembilan and several of the *orang baik* in the coffee shops. He was able soon thereafter to attend a feast in the *balaisa* celebrating the Prophet's birth. He stressed the fact that he desired to work with the whole community in the matter of educating its children, and, initially, received strong support from the villagers. On the first day of his teaching only thirty students appeared, about the same number as usual. However, by the end of his first week of teaching attendance had risen to more than sixty pupils.

This teacher, unlike his predecessor, gave subject matter instruction in the Malay language. He devoted a certain period each day to lessons in the Thai language, during which he stressed conversation—he was strict in his prohibition of any spoken Malay at this time. The curriculum reported in 1956 included the following subjects: Thai history, geography, reading and writing (in Thai), dictation (in Thai), arithmetic (largely memorization of tables), Buddhist morals, drawing, handicrafts, and physical training. In the last two grades bookkeeping and letter writing were added. By 1964, units on science and health and sanitation had been added. A unit on Buddhist morals and the previous requirement of honoring an image of the Buddha could not be expected to meet the approval of Muslim villagers and particularly their religious leaders. In part this is the cause of the basic hostility of the religious community in South Thailand toward secular education. While the broad curriculum guidelines are established in Bangkok, there is considerable latitude in local interpretation. On this basis, modifications have been made in the curriculum in Malay schools, such as the possibility of teaching in Malay, and the virtual abandonment of the unit on Buddhist morals. All that is required in the South now is that children be taught to know "good from bad." A further step toward decreasing Malay resistance to the curriculum has been the inclusion as part of the history offering of a short survey of the history of Islam and of the Malay people. While it appears that a step backward was taken by replacing Sunday as the legal holiday in South Thailand, in the school this was somewhat offset by allowing the three major Muslim holidays and the entire month of Ramadan as school holidays. It is the responsibility of the teacher before these recesses to explain (in Malay) the significance of each.

In recent years the central government has become aware of the serious need for good language instruction programs in the Malay-speaking area of Thailand. To help develop such programs a General Educational Development Centre was established in Yala staffed by Thais and Malays with advanced training in education. Among the experimental programs developed is an intensive course for primary grade language teachers. In the school used to test the program, teachers were given a month-long seminar-type course, and were then sent into the classroom to work with the students. Enthusiasm grew among both students and teachers, and enrollment almost doubled in the school during the second year of the experiment. It was found that 90 percent of the students instructed under this program developed a working vocabulary in Thai of at least six hundred words in two months. This vocabulary was confined on the whole to practical words, stressing situations that the students might encounter at school, in the market, and at home. As an incentive to learning Thai, a prize was offered each year to the best first grade student and teacher. Among the problems encountered by this experimental program, the most universal has been improper pronunciation: Malay is a language characterized by little change in tone or stress; Thai is characterized by a tonal system the misuse of which may altogether change the meaning of a word. In addition, Thai contains a number of sounds totally foreign to Malay speakers. However, the staff of the Yala Centre felt that as long as the students could make themselves understood in

Thai (and understand Thai speakers) the finer points of pronunciation could be sacrificed. Because of the unpopularity on the part of Thai teachers of living in the South, and the absolute scarcity of Malay teachers, both the quantity and the quality of teachers to be trained in this method were insufficient. Perhaps the most serious problem to the continuation and expansion of the program was resistance encountered at the district level. Although the work of the General Educational Development Centre has the whole-hearted support of the Ministry of Education (as well as international organizations), it is the provincial and district authorities who must make personnel, materials, and funds available in the experimental schools. In certain districts these officials, presumably interested in maintaining the *status quo,* are decidedly not cooperative. As one staff member of the Centre put it "the program has everything it needs except executive teeth." In Pattani, the provincial authorities encourage, in fact require, periodic courses for improvement in Thai language teaching methods of its teachers. These are short courses constantly circulating through the districts of the province. One teacher from each school in the district must attend during the week that the course is held in that district.

In spite of the increasing accommodation in the curriculum toward the special needs of the Malay Muslims of South Thailand, and in spite of the villagers' profession of the value of general education and the importance of learning to speak, read, and write Thai, there is still resistance toward government education, and attendance figures among Malay children continue to be low. *Orang baik* in Rusembilan recognize this fact and they furthermore recognize that usually it is attributed, often without justification, to the inadequacies of a village teacher. Considerable lip service is paid to the value of education, particularly in enabling an individual to compete effectively outside of the Malay villages, but parents rarely insist on their children going to school. Some parents go so far as to pay 200–300 *baht* ($10–15) to have their child's name removed from the school attendance rosters.

A large part of this resistance stems from the conservative Muslim element of the village population, personified chiefly by the Imam. As has been seen, the Imam of Rusembilan encourages children to miss school in order to devote more time to their religious studies. In spite of urging by the district officer, the Imam will not announce during Friday services that parents should make greater efforts to see that their children get to school. Several religious leaders in the village refuse to allow their children to attend the school. One religious leader even made the comment that he felt education made a man unreligious: "Literacy enables a man to disobey God. Civilization is antireligious." The village attitude toward a student who seriously pursues secular education is that he is losing a certain amount of his religious strength, that he is being contaminated by alien (Buddhist) ideas, to his ultimate detriment.

All the factors militating against the full acceptance of primary education are intensified when it comes to secondary education. Only one boy from Rusembilan has ever completed the eight secondary grades, and very few have ever started them. In addition to language barriers and basic religious resistance, transportation and cost become factors in secondary schooling. Rusembilan is fortunate in being within 3 miles of secondary schools in Pattani. Most villages are not. In 1952, out of 189 schools in Pattani province only three were secondary schools. While the total number of schools in the province had risen by more than 50 percent by 1960, the proportion of secondary schools had not increased. Tuition in the Pattani secondary school is 240 *baht* ($12) per year, in addition to which parents must provide their children with uniforms, shoes, books, paper, and pencils amounting to another 200 or 300 *baht* a year. This is often too much for village budgets to afford. However, secondary education remains one of the two major roads to upward mobility among Malays of South Thailand. It is the road by which Malays are able to participate in the apparatus of government, and to enter Thai official society on a surprisingly equal footing.

The other road to upward mobility remains entirely within the context of Islamic Malay society. This is higher religious education. In 1960 there were 133 *pondok*, or secondary religious schools, in Pattani province, and these offered direct competition in terms of Malay students to the government secondary schools. In 1956, it was estimated that as many as 80 percent of the youths of Rusembilan attended one of these *pondok* for at least a short period of time after their *Masuk Jawi*. They receive further instruction in proper performance of ritual and prayer, as well as additional details of Islamic Law. A few students, however, continue their studies for several years, hopefully make the pilgrimage to Mecca, and return to South Thailand as religious teachers or village Imams themselves. These students seek an understanding of Islam, not just a knowledge of its forms. In addition to this broader understanding, secondary level courses in history (Islamic), geography, and science are taught, although these are not considered to be essential to the education of a religious man. Language instruction has traditionally played an important part in the curriculum of the *pondok*, for only through a reading knowledge of Arabic could a student hope to acquire insight into the meaning of the Koran and other sacred books. Recently, the Thai government has decreed that instruction in the Thai language must be given to all those students at the *pondok* who are not already proficient in it (proficiency is presumed if the student has passed the first secondary grade of the government school). In addition, there is increasing instruction in English—in one *pondok* English is offered as an *alternative* to Arabic. In this school, the headmaster feels that English is an important modern language and has brought an instructor from Bangkok to teach it in a scientific fashion.

The daily round in the *pondok* begins with bathing, prayers, and a simple meal. By seven or eight o'clock the students gather in groups for reading and explanation of books by their teachers, or *guru*. Depending on the *guru* this will either be in the form of unison recitation and rote memorization by the students, or an attempt at meaningful explanation of the subject with questioning and discussion on the part of the students. This instruction, which lasts until noon, deals mostly with Islam and Islamic studies, but once or twice a week is devoted to the study of academic subjects. In the afternoon, from about two until five o'clock, language instruction is given. A portion of this period every day is devoted to instruction in Arabic in most of the *pondok*, while Thai, standard Malay, or English are offered as electives three times a week. The basic goals of this education are to provide the student with a direct knowledge of God; to teach him the principles of Islamic Law, particularly as it relates to marriage, divorce, and the division of property; and to insure proper management of his daily life including prayer and general conduct according to religious standards. Some *pondok* place greater emphasis on philosophical studies of the nature of man and his relationship with the world. None attaches great importance to academic studies as such.

Attendance at a *pondok* costs the parents about 1500 *baht* ($75), considerably more than the secondary school tuition. However, because of the religious value of this education, many parents are willing to sacrifice for it. Life at a typical *pondok* was described in the 1956 study of Rusembilan as follows (Fraser 1960: 160–61):

> The schools are constructed on a monastic plan. There is one building larger than the others in which instruction is held if it cannot be out of doors. The *guru* (teachers) and the *murid* (students) alike live two or three together in small elevated houses encircling the school. Often the residents of the school raise some kind of crops for use at the school or occasionally for sale. Ordinarily, a student will have to beg for the food he prepares for himself daily, though part of a person's *zakat* can be given for the support of religious students. The student is not supposed to have money with him at school which he might use for buying food; he may not smoke; and in general he is expected to live an ascetic life.[1]

There is no ceremony marking the conclusion of studies at the *pondok*. This is due to the fact that there is neither a fixed body of knowledge to be acquired nor a standard amount of time for learning it. Most *pondok* students return to their villages after a year or two, marry, and take up normal village occupations. The students who stay on for further study expect to journey to Mecca when they conclude their studies. Therefore either marriage or celebration of a man's pilgrimage can be considered as marking the conclusion of a youth's life as a student in the *pondok*.

Adult Status: A Resolution of Contradictions

Throughout the preceding pages, considerable attention has been devoted to what appears to be a basic difference in value systems characterizing traditional Malay aspects of village culture, on the one hand, and Islamic aspects, on the other. Each individual growing up in Rusembilan and similar villages is exposed to both of these systems, although their respective intensities may vary markedly in individual cases. However, the average villager gives little or no thought to any contradictions which may be inherent in his own set of values. Only rarely is he aware of them in the community at large, as in disagreements over the value of secular education, or in the attitudes of the religious leaders concerning dealings with *hantu* and jinns. In a sense, the activities of Rusembilan are com-

[1] © 1960 by Cornell University. Used by permission of Cornell University Press.

partmentalized, with a minimum of overlap except in the case of those men who act as leaders of the community.

Economic activities, especially fishing, occupy a large part of an adult's time. These activities are guided by a set of values stressing personal industry, avoidance of trouble to others, adherence to the rules of tradition, and the positive attraction of wealth. Within the limits set by one's relations with others, competition is an important element in economic pursuits. Owners and steerers of *kolek* seek to recruit the best crew possible, as crewmen seek the most successful *kolek*. Competition between *kolek* is accepted, and each boat attempts to return to shore earlier than the others so that its crew may take advantage of the somewhat higher fish prices early in the morning. Because of this, considerable difficulty was experienced during the season when Rusembilan fishermen experimented with motor tow boats which required synchronization of the activities of two or three *kolek*. Land and plantation ownership has traditionally been an individual matter, each owner attempting, with as little reliance on others as possible, to exploit his holding efficiently and profitably. Within the nuclear family there is a minimum of subordination of individual members to the family group. Women are accorded respect on the basis of their accomplishments almost commensurate with men. Even children are given consideration as individuals rather than as simply members of a group. Whatever money a child earns as a result of performing small tasks for other villagers is his. His parents may advise him about safeguarding and careful spending, but the child retains ultimate control.

With few exceptions, the Malay villager is a sincere adherent to Islam. This adherence ordinarily demands relatively little effort or attention on the part of the villager. Essentially all that Islam has added to the traditional Malay cultural substratum is the obligation to pray five times a day, the expectation of a certain amount of time spent in religious instruction, a month of fasting, and a number of feast days. Religious instruction and the month-long fast are obviously more time consuming and, in a sense, more burdensome than prayer and feasting. However, there is little conflict between fasting and fishing, one is a daytime activity, the other done at night. If religious instruction appears to be coming into conflict with the beginning of a youth's fishing career, religious instruction is ceased forthwith. In spite of the Imam's demands to the contrary, fishermen of Rusembilan have begun fishing on Thursday night. The average villager is a sincere believer, but Islam is worn lightly.

To the villager, Islam means a subordination of his own individuality in certain defined situations. Among the values given by the Imam of Rusembilan are a knowledge of God (as an omnipotent lawgiver), and of the Law, and a readiness to follow the leadership of the Imam and other important religious persons. Villagers often comment that in religious matters one should not seek reasons, but do as one is told. Services in the mosque, like instruction in religious schools, consist of statements of authority by the Imam or *guru*, followed by unison recitation of the response by the congregation or the students. What is outside of the context of religion as specified by the Koran, or secondary by interpretative works, is of indifference to or even in conflict with the values of religion.

A third set of values, harder to confine to a particular area of activity, falls somewhere between the villager's economic individualism and his religious subordination. These values, stressing generosity, helpfulness, and cooperation, are more in evidence in interior villages where they pertain to the dominant economic activity, rice cultivation. Such values become important in matters where solidarity of the community or of a family group within the community is threatened. The assistance expected and received by family members, as when an aging couple can no longer provide for itself, or before a new couple becomes established, calls on these values. Also they are characteristic of the *orang baik* of the community, even though these men have acquired their status primarily through individualistic economic activity.

While most villagers are guided in their behavior by some combination of these values, a few, characteristically religious leaders, stress one set almost to the exclusion of the others. Occasionally, such overemphasis is found in an individual who has no particular status that might demand it. These individuals are considered as oddities within the community. The two following examples illustrate two extremes of this aberrant value emphasis. One man, a relative of the Rusembilan *kamnan,* supports himself by tending the fighting bulls of a Chinese merchant in Pattani. During the fishing season (which is also the bull fighting season) this man occupies his entire time feeding, grooming, and accompanying the bulls to their fights (in this type of bull fighting, one bull fights another). During the monsoon season he cultivates a small rice field which he can manage without the assistance of others. His behavior is unsocial, on several occasions he has resorted to beating other individuals to gain what he wanted. While he has made a considerable amount of money during his career, he is not now particularly well-off because of frequent damage suits. He is neither liked by nor associated with by other villagers. The second example concerns a very fine carpenter in Rusembilan. This man's behavior is guided by the desire to cause no one the slightest trouble or harm. Frequently, his property is stolen, but he refuses to take any action toward detecting the thief or recovering the property. Other villagers recognize that the values underlying his behavior are simply exaggerations of some of their own, but they feel that this man is foolish for not properly balancing one set against the other.

As was indicated in the previous chapter, all ceremonial occasions in Rusembilan with the partial exception of those connected specifically with the Islamic calendar can be seen as attempting to serve and to harmonize these different and potentially divisive values. The intertwining of these values in the life crisis rituals was indicated. The *makan pulot,* important in almost every ceremonial event, further illustrates the concurrent operation of different sets of values within a single ceremonial or social framework. Not only is this feast specifically held to elaborate or intensify a particular ceremonial event, often within the Islamic religious context, but it reaffirms other values as well. Seen as a fulfillment of obligations to family, community, and regional connections, it recognizes those values stressing generosity, helpfulness, and cooperation. In this light, also, the *makan pulot* functions as community entertainment. Seen as a public display of resources, it recognizes individualistic and competitive values. These are also primary in both the attempt to give larger and larger *makan pulot,* and the efforts made to show a profit at the end. The *makan pulot* can also be seen as reasserting the religious (and social) status of subordination and superordination, with its formal requirement of inviting religious leaders and *orang baik* first.

Conflicting sets of values cause most trouble at the level of community leadership. Here a man, in a sense, remains within the public eye, and his actions are judged by the status he holds. When the Imam of Rusembilan became involved in commercial activities, such as buying motor boats and running a rice mill, he was severely criticized by villagers. His prestige as a religious leader suffered to the extent that he gave rein to a set of values inappropriate to that status. An *orang baik,* a leader in secular affairs, must be a good Muslim, but his leadership does not ordinarily extend into the area of religion. In fact, too great an emphasis on Islamic values is apt to reflect unfavorably upon the status of the *orang baik.* Villagers whose lives combine the different values expect to find them clearly separated in their leaders.

In 1956, the villagers of Rusembilan said, "The young men today are diligent: when the prawns are gone, they go out for *kembong,* and during the rains they catch fish along the shore. Today, everyone has money all the time, not just when there are *kembong.* The young men today are better than we were —they like to talk about religion and to go to *makan pulot.* They know that religion is good, especially in hard times." (Fraser 1960: 248.) Times have become harder since 1956 with a marked decrease in the availability of *kembong,* and there is a noticeable tendency in the coastal villages to place greater stress on the importance of religion and religious values. It is almost as if values characteristic of the economic sphere of activity were being discarded as no longer of use. On the other hand, through developmental programs and emphasis on primary education and linguistic instruction, the Thai government appears to be making itself more evident in Malay villages in the South. The most readily available means of signifying his distinctiveness in the face of increasing contact with the Thais is the Malay villager's membership in the Islamic world community. He is unable to rally around linguistic differences, for these are under direct attack by the government. Although he insists he is first a Malay and then a Muslim, he is unable to use his Malay culture as a mark of distinctiveness, for either he is branded as an irredentist, or he is unable to define clearly what the distinctive elements of Malay culture are—other than religion. Religious and traditional values are not in conflict at all points, however. Both can be pursued: for example, religious and traditional values both encourage personal diligence. While religious instruction has tended in the past to emphasize formal or routine matters of religion, such as memorization of the Koran and the proper forms for prayer, there is a growing conflict between the religious views of young and old. Younger men, some exposed to the newer teaching methods at the *pondok,* are demanding and often achieving a deeper and fuller understanding of the meaning of the Koran, and of Islam in general.

7

The Changing Scene

Technological Change and Community Integration

B ECAUSE OF THE DEGREE of compartmentalization of values in Rusembilan, changes in the economic sphere of the culture tend to be able to occur with a maximum of freedom from screening by values associated with other areas of the culture. That such changes may eventually, through adaptation to them, cause conflict with other parts of the culture is rarely, if ever, an initial consideration of the villagers. The series of innovations in the fishing operations of Rusembilan between 1956 and 1960 is illustrative of this readiness to change without due regard for possible disruptive consequences. A detailed account of the first stages of this series of innovations is given in the 1956 study of Rusembilan (Fraser 1960: 249–258) which indicates, among other things, how decisions are reached at Rusembilan, the role of the *orang baik* in the process, and sense of village disapproval at the Imam's major role in an area where he should not have been involved. This account is summarized below.

Prior to the *kembong* season of 1956, fishing boats from Rusembilan relied entirely on sails and oars to take them from the village to the fishing grounds and back. Actually, the use of oars represented a fairly recent innovation: Rusembilan was one of the few villages in the east coast area of South Thailand which had given up forward-facing paddling for rear-facing rowing. Prior to this fishing season, there had been a good deal of general talk about the advantages of using some form of motor to facilitate getting to the fishing grounds. No nearby fishing villages had experimented with motorization and it was therefore difficult for the Rusembilan villagers to assess realistically the advantages and disadvantages of different types of motorization. These conversations, usually between only two or three boat owners and steerers, culminated early in the fishing season, in a general meeting (following a small religious feast) in the *balaisa*. While one steerer talked in favor of outfitting individual *kolek* with outboard motors at a cost of under 6000 *baht* ($300), the others considered that a smaller number of motor launches each able to tow two or three *kolek* would be preferable. Estimates of the cost of these launches ranged from 18,000 to 60,000 *baht* ($900–$3000). There was much discussion as to how financing could be arranged, alternative methods of procuring the boats, and the fact that village fishermen would have to work extra time in order to justify the expenditure. However, no clear consensus was reached at the meeting.

During the two weeks that followed the meeting, groups of two or three owners and steerers again dominated the deliberations. However, these groups tended to become stabilized in their composition. Men who were particularly friendly; who had economic relationships with each other, such as steering and owning the same boat or jointly owning a boat; or who patronized the same coffee shop, would frequently meet and discuss details of financing and use of motor launches. One of these groups consisted of the Imam and his father-in-law (between them owning two *kolek*), the steerer of the Imam's *kolek,* and the steerer's brother who owned and steered his own boat. Over the initially mild objections of the Imam's father-in-law, the other members of the group, apparently having reached no definite decision, set off to buy a motor launch. It is reported that the Imam, himself, entered into negotiations with a merchant in Nakorn Sritamarat and purchased a boat with only the most cursory inspection (it was later maintained that this group had decided that at the very least the motor of the launch should be checked over by a competent mechanic). On the way back to Rusembilan by sea the crankcase of the engine developed a serious crack and the boat had to be towed in. Three days after the crippled launch reached Rusembilan, *Pak Sa* purchased a smaller launch, also from Nakorn Sritamarat. During the weeks that followed, the engine of the "Imam's launch" (*mutu Imam*) was repaired three separate times, each time the crack reopened. At last it was decided to invest over 20,000 *baht* ($1000) in a new engine. (The purchase price of the boat had been 40,000 *baht*.) *Pak Sa* was complaining during this time that the advantages of launches did not outweigh their cost: his was particularly slow. He announced that he would like to sell his launch. Within six weeks of the original purchase, two additional launches had been bought by groups of Rusembilan fishermen, bringing the total to four.

By the last third of the 1956 fishing season, eleven of the twelve Rusembilan *kolek* has made arrangements of one sort or another to be included in the tow group of one of the motor launches. It was then that the disruptive consequences began to be apparent. Basically, the problem was that membership in a tow group meant that the individual *kolek* and their steerers were deprived of a considerable amount of their previous independence in locating fish and in timing their return to market them. Disputes arose almost immediately over the position of particular *kolek* in the tow as the last boat in the string was dropped off at the first-sighted school of mackerel, often giving it a large advantage over the other *kolek*. This problem was solved relatively easily, although never to the satisfaction of all, by rotating positions each night. A more difficult problem arose in regard to the return trip. Frequently one *kolek* in a tow group would have caught a full load of fish while the other *kolek* desired to fish further. Neither the alternative of waiting idly while the other *kolek* finished fishing and while the market prices might be dropping, nor that of rowing back to shore ahead of the tow was particularly appealing. The second alternative was most often chosen with the result, in a number of cases, that the last boats to finish fishing would be towed in and overtake those which had left the fishing area earlier.

Once on shore the problems did not end. The system of distribution used initially by the Imam's and *Pak Sa's* tow groups involved a pooling of the total catch of the component *kolek* and division into equal shares for the crewmen with extra shares for steerers, *kolek* owners, the launch owners and "for the launch," or its fuel. After an early period of poor fishing for all, it became obvious to the wives of members of the "luckier," more skillful *kolek* that by this system they were in effect subsidizing the less successful crews. A great deal of acrimony in the village resulted, and on several occasions violence broke out (between women). Although a new distribution system was instituted whereby each *kolek* divided its own catch, and all paid a fixed amount in fish or in cash for the tow, a completely satisfactory solution was never reached. Now wives of members of the less successful crews complained that whereas they might have no fish to market they were compelled to pay as much for the tow as were crews (and wives) of *kolek* in the same tow returning with full catches.

The effects of this situation in other areas of community life were apparent. Not only was there overt hostility on the part of the women, but relationships between men became noticeably strained. Even within a single *kolek* crew there were hard feelings as one man felt that his fellows were not standing up sufficiently to other crews, and another felt that there was too much of this kind of behavior. Attendance at the coffee shops fell off markedly during this period and, partly because of subsequent developments, has never fully recovered. Even religious leaders and *orang baik* were open to criticism by many of the villagers. The *orang baik* were particularly vulnerable because of the involvement of most of them in ownership and operation of the motor launches. As a consequence, the chief source of authority and means for maintaining community harmony was seriously undermined. Because most of the village's religious leaders were more aloof from the motor boats than were the *orang baik,* their status in the village increased.

By the following fishing season, 1957, *Pak Sa* had sold his launch and had equipped his two boats that had formed his tow group, with outboard motors. In addition, one *kolek* from each of two other tow groups had been equipped with outboard motors and were now fishing independently as was the single *kolek* which had not been part of a tow group in 1956. The only tow group to be left entirely intact was that of the Imam's launch. The Imam, himself, with the assistance of one of his crewmen took on the job of running and maintaining the launch, although neither had particular skill or experience in mechanical matters. As a consequence, the Imam was forced to give up his duties in religious instruction. All of the Koran classes in Rusembilan were now conducted by the Imam's wife. Although the Imam's religious knowledge and competence in leading ritual was never questioned by the villagers, his status as a religious *leader* in the community and exemplar of religious values suffered a further blow from this increased involvement with secular, economic affairs.

At the end of the 1959 fishing season, the Imam disposed of the last remaining motor launch in Rusembilan. Parenthetically, his leadership position was hardly benefited by this as he soon thereafter began operating his rice mill. By now all *kolek* at Rusembilan were equipped with outboard motors, as were a number of the smaller village boats. Official boat registration figures are of interest in this regard. In 1956 in the four Malay provinces of Thailand only eighteen motorized boats were officially registered while 224 nonmotorized boats (boats smaller then *kolek* need not be registered) were registered. In 1960, the number of motorized boats (any boat with a motor must be registered) was 553, while only seven remained in the unmotorized category. The apparent doubling of the boat population in South Thailand is due in part to the requirement of registering any motorized boat regardless of size, and in part to the fact that it is harder to evade registration officials if one's *kolek* is motorized then if it is not.

This reindividualization of village fishing helped in restoring good relations in Rusembilan. However, the previous degree of community integration based on boat crew membership and leadership and authority by *orang baik* whose status largely depended on boat group affiliation was not regained. Fishing operations had essentially changed. A minor innovation in 1960 ended all necessity for crew coactivity ashore. This was the substitution of nylon for cotton gill nets. Prior to this series of innovations beginning with the tow launches, boat crews would assemble a half an hour before launching, carefully remove the nets from the drying racks, and stow them in the boat; sails were inspected, and oars readied. As the boat set out to sea a common *esprit* existed, a common question as to the duration of offshore breezes, and a common desire that it continue, saving the crewmen from rowing. After raising and lowering the heavier cotton nets several times in filling the *kolek* with fish, the men would ply their oars together for the return trip. While the women distributed the fish on the beach, it was the task of the crew members jointly to unload the net and spread it to dry, checking for tears which would require immediate attention. Today a *kolek* crew arrives at the boat just before it is to be launched for the night's work. Under way, they relax or sleep. At this point, and on the return trip there is no necessary work for anyone but the steerer. Casting and hauling the nylon net is a job that can be handled easily by five men (rather than the nine or ten who were required with cotton nets). Once on the beach with its catch, the crew disbands, leaving the net in place ready for the next fishing trip. There has been a conscious decision at Rusembilan to keep *kolek* crews larger than the necessary minimum to accomplish the fishing job. Such featherbedding coupled with a consistent decline in the availability of fish since 1960 has undermined the sense of pride formerly characteristic of the crews of successful *kolek* (and the sense of competing as a single group against the better boats, characteristic of the less-successful *kolek*). This undermining and loosening of group solidarity has also carried over to the status of the steerer as a man of great skill and knowledge, and, as already seen, to his status in the community at large.

Related in a number of ways to these developments is the decline in attendance at the coffee shops, and a basic change in their social function. The most widely given reason for this decline is the scarcity of money. But perhaps two other factors play as important a part. One of these is the loosening of group solidarity of the boat crews, mentioned above. Not only do the crew members feel less a part of a group than they did in the past, but their actual physical to-getherness once on shore (the spreading and mending of nets) is no longer required. Likewise, the steerers and owners are no longer the center of a group whose identity could in the past easily have been recognized, whether at sea or in the coffee shop. As pointed out earlier, people are now drawn to coffee shops because they expect to find people there talking about particular topics of inter-est to them, no longer because their comrades and their own economic leaders are there. Thus, while in the past the coffee shops served as foci of village au-thority and decision making because of the regular presence of one or more *orang baik* in each one, they are now more in the nature of centers of gossip. The exception to this is the coffee shop run by the father-in-law of the Imam which is frequented by other religious leaders, and in the increasingly important area of religious activities and values, functions much as in the past. The *orang baik* themselves, now less accessible, their economic perspicacity now taken less for granted, appear gradually to be losing their position of authority in the com-munity to the group of religious leaders who (except for the Imam) have nei-ther been victimized by circumstance, nor acted in any manner open to criticism.

Economic Change: From Sea to Jungle

One of the factors leading to decreasing the former solidarity of *kolek* crews and generally reducing community cohesion was a steady decrease in the supply of major species of fish, notably *kembong,* in the waters accessible to vil-lage craft. From a total yield in the four Malay provinces of Thailand of nearly 9000 metric tons of fish in 1956, yield had dropped to just over 4000 tons in 1960 and to under 3000 in 1963. This is not a purely local phenomenon. The fishing industry along the east coast of peninsular Malaysia has been similarly affected. Malaysian fishery officials attribute the condition to minor shifts in wind and sea currents which have caused the large concentrations of plankton on which the fish feed to drift further offshore. There seems to be no reduction in the numbers of fish, but simply a change in their accessibility to village fisher-men. The fishermen of Rusembilan, however, believe that the situation is being caused by an absolute diminution of the number of fish; and this they lay squarely on the large-scale, highly capitalized fishing operations which have in-creasingly in recent years been netting in the waters of the lower Gulf of Thai-land and the South China Sea. Although villagers allege that such fishing is in the hands of Chinese, they also consider that the Thai government is involved in some form of subsidization or sponsorship. They have little knowledge of the details of such fishing activities other than knowing that the large ships used have refrigeration facilities and that the nets used are large, expensive, and effective. They also blame these fishing enterprises for flooding the local market with fish and substantially lowering the price. Actually, although there has been a decline in the price of *kembong* due to increasing supplies from the west coast, other species have brought surprisingly constant prices throughout the period between 1956 and 1962—it is these other species which are sought by the commercial fishing boats. However, regardless of the actual facts of the situation, the fishermen of Rusembilan are convinced of their interpretation and consequently base their behavior on it.

Ideally, they would like to compete on the same scale. Practically, they realize that village resources could never enable them to purchase the equipment necessary. The development of compromise, medium-scale fishing by villagers, usually in partnership with town merchants, has been discussed in Chapter 2. There is a growing number of such arrangements in South Thailand, and a growing realization that they present to the average crewman a profitable alternative to traditional fishing. However, neither their development nor the interest in them as a possible occupation is growing fast enough at present to make up for the declining economies of the coastal villages. As one resident of Rusembilan remarked in 1960, "there is no longer laughter in the village."

Decreasing village income, coupled with unnecessarily large *kolek* crews, has forced a number of village families to seek economic alternatives to *kembong* fishing in order to subsist. These families represent the lower socio-economic levels of the villages. They have never been particularly successful *kembong* fishermen, they do not own much, if any, land for rice or coconut growing, and they have never been numbered among the important families in the village. Usually, the first alternative to *kembong* fishing is a traditional one, small-scale inshore fishing. In 1956, there was a total of fourteen small boats used for this type of fishing in Rusembilan. In addition three or four families fished exclusively by wading in the shallow waters near shore. By 1964, the number of small boats had more than doubled, and six or seven families fished more or less regularly in shallow water. While the profits from this type of fishing are small (one person can make only about 1 or 2 *baht* per day) they are regular, and with both man and wife and sometimes other family members working, sufficient income can be produced to live adequately if not comfortably.

Another alternative sought by a number of coastal villagers is that of working for wages in a capital town. In Rusembilan, there are now three men who make their living carrying passengers in three-wheeled, pedal-operated rickshaws. These men operate their vehicles in Pattani during the day and return to Rusembilan in the evening, bringing a fare with them if they can. Another three men from Rusembilan are employed as coolies by the Pattani municipal government, and one man has been hired by the bus company which operates between Pattani and Rusembilan to maintain the village road. While this represents only a small proportion of the population of Rusembilan, it represents an important increase over 1956 when no villager was so employed. In fact, at that time people from Rusembilan would often hire laborers from outside the village to do heavy work for them. While wages for town employment are somewhat better than the income from shallow water fishing, the standard of living of these employees is no better than that of the marginal fishermen since they must purchase all of their food.

The most significant economic alternative to *kembong* fishing at this time involves working in one capacity or another in inland portions of the area on fruit- and rubber-producing properties. Rubber tapping for hire, although not a particularly congenial occupation for coastal villagers, now accounts for the greatest number of people (in 1960 only one man was so employed). Not only can man and wife work as a team and realize a good profit, but by working for someone else they avoid the complexities of acquiring their own land, and, probably most important, do not commit themselves permanently to a life in the interior. They are free to come and go as they please, and, although many are being economically forced to spend greater amounts of time at tapping, there is still the conviction among coastal villagers that *kembong* fishing cannot get worse than it is and that it must therefore get better.

Actual ownership of rubber-producing land by coastal villagers is not new. However, between 1956 and 1964 there were significant differences in both the type of person who acquired rubber land and how the land was acquired. At the earlier time, the only men from Rusembilan who owned such land were wealthy individuals, often numbered among the *orang baik* of the community. These men invested in rubber land as they would in coconut plantations or in *kolek,* capital goods which could be maintained and utilized by the owner when he chose and by others the rest of the time. They found, however, that being based in a coastal village far from their rubber plantations, they themselves were neither able to take care of their properties, nor supervise others. In fact, it would have been difficult to find labor for maintaining these lands, as at that time, none was producing rubber. Because of such difficulties most of the rubber-growing property owned by individuals from Rusembilan in 1956 has been sold. The new group of rubber landholders, on the other hand, are universally *not* wealthy individuals. They are people being forced into alternative occupations by the decline in fishing. They are not people, like the earlier owners, who have definite status in the village as well as capital goods and relatives located there. And they are decidedly not acquiring rubber lands as a form of capital investment, rather they are going into rubber as a means of supporting themselves and their families. In 1956, acquisition of interior land by villagers from Rusembilan involved either payment to the government (or a former private owner) or settlement of a previous owner's delinquent taxes. Today, the most usual means of acquiring this land is to squat on it—to start improving it immediately *and* continuously. In similar fashion, a number of coastal villagers have availed themselves of the government's formalized "squatting" or resettlement programs in the area. Thus the basic difference that appeared between 1956 and 1964 is that while the earlier owners, anchored in many ways to their coastal village, sought interior land as *another* way of investing capital, the new owners have staked everything on their plantations and have severed all ties, economic, social, and religious, with their former coastal villages. If these latter do not succeed at rubber growing, they will be left with nothing to fall back on. Therefore, it is reasonable to assume, as long as world rubber prices do not fall to much below their present level, that these people have made a permanent transition from fishing to plantation management and that others will be forced by the same reasons to do likewise.

A final effect of the deteriorating coastal economic situation can be seen in the patterns of living in the villages themselves. As indicated in Chapter 3, the simple nuclear family of parents and children is the basic unit of this society. It is also the preferred residential unit. It is true that newly married couples ordinarily live for a time with one or both sets of parents and that aging couples spend their declining years with their children. But most families consider these arrangements as only temporary interruptions in the normal pattern of living as a separate nuclear unit. Although the population of Rusembilan rose by almost exactly 25 percent between 1956 and 1964, the total number of residential units rose by less than 2 percent. The cause of this situation is clearly economic. Houses are expensive to build, and money is in short supply. This is not to say that no new houses have been built since 1956: twenty have been, but during the same period eighteen houses have been taken down or allowed to fall to pieces—most of these belonging to emigrants from the village. The average size of each Rusembilan household has risen from just under six and one-half persons to eight. In 1956, simple nuclear families consisting of one married couple and their children accounted for 61 percent of Rusembilan households. By 1964, only 50 percent of Rusembilan households contained only a single nuclear family. On the other hand, the proportion of joint families (having more than one married couple *on the same generational level*) rose during this period from 6 to 11 percent of the total households in Rusembilan. While these statistics may not be conclusive, they are certainly indicative of the economic pressures.

The Government and Planned Change

Until recently, economic development programs have lagged in the South of Thailand both for economic and for political reasons. The economic reasons simply were that the South as a region was economically as well off as any in the country, and it still is. The political reasons, which will be dealt with in the following section, had to do with the problems arising in certain districts of the north and northeast bordering on Loas. As far as the central government is concerned, the South does not present any serious economic problems because of its exportable rubber and rice surpluses. It does present a potentially serious problem of political security. During the past five or six years considerable economic development activity has been initiated in South Thailand. Yala, the center of this activity, now boasts the General Educational Development Centre, a community development training school, as well as a number of other more specialized agencies all working on problems in the South.

Following the example of other developing nations and using the existing administrative hierarchy of village, *tambon*, district, province and nation, the Thai government has instituted a nationwide community development program. The basic unit in this structure is the village committee, members of which serve on the *tambon* committee. The *tambon* committee is the direct out-growth of the *tambon* councils instituted by the administrative hierarchy in 1956 (see Chapter 4). Thus the community development program in Thailand had, in comparison with some countries, an initial head start. The organizational framework was there. While the program has advanced further in other areas of Thailand, it is well established in the South and is expected to expand rapidly. A basic problem here, as in other areas of contact between the villagers of the South and the government, is the language barrier. Until the opening of the community development training center in Yala, community development workers were recruited largely from other parts of Thailand and were acquainted neither with Malay culture nor language. The goals are standard: to increase peasant productivity through more efficient techniques, better plant and animal varieties, feed and fertilizer, and through diversification if necessary; to improve transportation, sanitation, housing, and appearance of villages; and to encourage self-identity, self-reliance, and solidarity among the villagers. In 1964, in Pattani and Yala provinces, community development projects (each covering an entire *amphur* or district) were confined to those areas with relatively large concentrations of Thai-speaking population; in Narathiwat work was going on among predominantly Malay-speaking villagers.

The community development project in Khok Pho district of Pattani province is typical of interior projects in areas of sizeable but not exclusive Thai-speaking population. There the village workers report generally good response. In one village of this district, however, people won't come to evening meetings called by the worker as they fear the activities of thugs or bandits in the neighborhood—and are unable to get sufficient police protection. Otherwise, attendance at and participation in these meetings are said to be good. One village worker asserts that Thai-speaking villagers carry on all discussion themselves and reach decisions concerning program matters (always within the framework of the government program) for the greatest good of the whole village. The Malay villagers in this area, however, do not participate well in these discussions, although the village worker officially speaks Malay. The village worker attributes this to the inability on the part of the Malays to understand the aims of the program. On the other hand, the Malay villagers are characterized by being much easier for the village worker to work with. They are more docile; they will do what they are told to do.

Among the programs carried out within this district project, most have been concerned with construction of roads and culverts and with agricultural diversification. A few community centers have been constructed, but these function for the most part as housing for the village worker. Some attempt has been made to organize women's sewing groups, but whatever interest is generated in this usually is vitiated by the infrequency of the visits of the single female worker in the district. The biggest developmental effort in this district has been encouragement of coffee growing by the villagers (and a related restriction of planting rights on nearby government forest reserve). Although recent figures are not available, the trend in coffee production in South Thailand between 1959 and 1961 was in the direction of a marked decline in both acreage and yields. This is in spite of the government requirement that domestic coffee make up at least 15 percent of the total purchases of wholesale coffee dealers in the country. At best, a low grade of coffee can be grown in South Thailand, and this requires clearing jungle, and cultivation and harvesting techniques alien to the local villagers. In spite of the efforts to increase coffee production as part of the community development program, there is still considerable surreptitious use of the reserved forests by villagers for growing fruit and small amounts of rubber.

It was proposed to initiate a community development project in a Malay-speaking coastal district of Pattani province during 1965. Government officials were enthusiastic about the possibilities of incorporating a shrimp-farming program into this project. This would involve breeding large and high-quality shrimp and prawns in a restricted area of the sea, facilitating high-yield fishing by villagers involved in the project. There was considerable skepticism among villagers concerning the technical competence of the government officials to undertake this project. Men of Rusembilan pointed with amusement at an agricultural development program initiated in their village by district agricultural officials (not connected with the national community development program). The goal of the program was to utilize the waste land between village *padi* fields for planting coconut trees. Ordinarily, the fields are separated by a narrow strip about 2 feet wide which serves to prevent water from running off the flooded fields, allows a certain amount of grazing area for village animals, and also provides a dry path for getting from one place to another. The coconut program started running into serious difficulties almost as soon as it was started. Who owned the trees? Traditionally a man owns his *padi* field, but not the dike between his field and the next. Disputes as to the ownership of coconuts arose long before there were any nuts to be harvested, and it is perhaps fortunate that the whole program was scrapped before the trees, and the disputes, came to fruition. Coconut trees have very shallow root systems, and with the trees planted a foot to 18 inches above the level of the rice fields, it became impossible to plow the fields near the dikes without either breaking the plows or the coconut roots. Furthermore, as the trees sought nutriment from the soil, this was depriving the rice plants with the result that within a 25- or 30-foot radius of a tree the rice did very poorly. The villagers also pointed to the out-of-season rice planting project initiated by the district officer in 1964 (see Chapter 2) as an example of the technical incompetence of government planners. While the shrimp-farming program may have considerable technical merit, its biggest problem will be in overcoming the skepticism built on prior experience, and in enlisting villagers' cooperation in its creation and utilization.

A more massive community development effort has been undertaken in a few areas of South Thailand, as well as in the North and Northeast of the country. This program under the direction of the Thai army involves the use of mobile development units. Such a unit with a large staff of officers and technicians, heavy mechanized equipment and communications facilities, moves into an area for a period of several months. Roads are bulldozed through the jungle, electricity, drainage, and water systems put in, often entire villages are reconstructed, and agricultural practices are completely revolutionized. After the initial phase. most of the unit moves on, leaving a cadre of officers and technicians to see that the "progressive" changes are maintained. The mobile development units undoubtedly bring about massive transition in the lives of villagers, and the indication is that there is relatively little back-sliding after the last of the development team leaves the area. Surprisingly, there seems to be a generally positive and favorable reaction on the part of the villagers to the activities of the mobile development units in the South. Perhaps their aggressive, intensive, and coordinated approach holds lessons for the national community development program organized along more standard lines.

In one other major sphere the Thai government has been carrying on developmental activity in South Thailand. This program, called Self-Help Land Settlements, involves relocation of families from other areas (local or far removed) on large tracts of land in unsettled and potentially productive areas. There are four such areas in the provinces of Pattani, Yala, Narathiwat, and an adjoining portion of Songkhla, with a total area of over a quarter of a million acres. Within each tract, 10-acre plots are demarcated as homesteads and are connected by roadways with the administrative headquarters of the settlement. One plot will be allotted to any family seeking resettlement with the requirement that this be developed over a period of five years. The ultimate objectives of the program are essentially the same as those of the community development program, with the advantage that all settlers start from scratch under the supervision of program officials and with the clearly understood stipulation that full title can be obtained only by proper and efficient management of the holding. Two other purposes are assumed to be served by the settlement program which are not part of community development activities as such. These are to halt a trend toward migration off poor lands to the congested urban areas of Bangkok by means of making available productive land at no cost, and to impress upon the rural population that the government has an active interest in their welfare. So far, the great majority of settlers in South Thailand are Thai-speakers from northern areas. The few Malay families which have availed themselves of such land offerings find the environment uncomfortable. Not only are the other settlers predominantly Thai, but there are rarely provisions for religious structures other than Buddhist, and distances to established village mosques are usually great. Probably the only significant use made of the settlement projects by Malay villagers will be in groups of families, similar to the settlement (next to but not on the project land) by the ten families from Rusembilan discussed in Chapter 2.

Minority Groups and National Security

While the villager responds to programs of community development and economic assistance in his area in terms of traditional economic and cultural values, the motives of the government in instituting such activities may be somewhat more complex. From the point of view of the government of Thailand, the

South is characterized by two problems: one is the old sore of Malay irredent-ism, the other a relatively recent threat of Communism. And while no one would deny that government programs in the South are in part motivated by sincere interest in economic development, it would be equally foolish to rule out political considerations as an important part of any such motivation.

As has already been pointed out, the provinces of Pattani, Yala, Narathi-wat, and Satun are populated by an overwhelming majority of Muslim peoples who are culturally Malay rather than Thai, and who, in the former three prov-inces, generally cannot communicate in the Thai language. From a third to a half of the non-Malay population consists of Chinese, either native or Thai-born. These Chinese, with political sympathies ranging from complete loyalty to Thailand through support of the Taipei republic to more or less active support of Peking, in large measure control the economy of the South (as they often do elsewhere). Neither the Malays, insisting on their distinctiveness, nor the Chi-nese, economically powerful and politically ambiguous, are conducive to official peace of mind in Bangkok. The situation is made somewhat more uncomfortable for the government by the fact that relations between the Chinese and Malays in the area are good. Government officials have in the past come into the area for short periods and left, often looking on their tour of duty in the South simply as an unpleasant interlude to be partially compensated for by whatever exploita-tive means were at hand. While less true of officials posted in technical capaci-ties such as agriculture and fisheries, the attitude is prevalent among Thai officials that the Malays are ignorant, incapable of understanding, and lacking in civilized attributes. Official attitudes in Bangkok, with varying degrees of strin-gency, have tended to reinforce the positions of local officials. In the extension of Thai influence, little or sometimes no toleration of non-Thai values or behav-ior was to be condoned.

"We are Malays; Thailand is not our country, it is over there." With phrases such as this, the Muslims of South Thailand seek to maintain and rein-force their distinctiveness, and to recall their glorious, and perhaps overglorified past as rulers of the territory now a part of an alien nation. This attitude is con-stantly just below the surface in every Malay village in South Thailand. It is po-tentially, and at times actually, a powerful disruptive force. However, either its mobilization or its control requires educated Malay leadership. In the past, par-ticularly during the fifteen years under the Phibun government, repressive gov-ernment policy has brought forth leadership of the first type: periodic explosive reactions by the Malays. As early as 1923, a widespread movement developed in the South as a reaction to the alleged funneling out of the area of a large share of the tax revenues collected from among the Malays. This movement started simply as resistance by not paying taxes, but soon had grown to a full-fledged movement for independence of the area from Thailand. This, like subsequent movements, required calling in of government military and police units and the detention (and usually execution) of the leaders to regain order. A series of similar movements characterized the period between the abolition of absolute monarchy in Thailand in 1932 and the period of the second World War and Phibun's cultural rules. Shortly after the war, an extensive organization developed in the South whose initial goal was the repeal of the distasteful conditions of the cultural rules, with the specific benefits for Malay Muslims mentioned in Chapter 4. Like the earlier tax protest movement, this movement also developed into something far more radical than originally planned. A petition was drafted and signed (or thumb printed) by a reported half of the adult Malay population of Pattani, Yala, and Narathiwat provinces. This petition, addressed to the United Nations, sought secession from Thailand of the three provinces and union with the Federation of Malaya. The leaders of this movement were apprehended early in 1948, but not before the petition received wide publicity in the world press. Large-scale fighting continued throughout the first half of 1948, requiring the mobilization of great numbers of government military and police troops in the area.

Since that time, although there have been no movements on the scale of that just mentioned, there have been frequent small irredentist uprisings, each calling for restoration of order by the military. Since the independence of the Federation of Malaya in 1957 and the outlawing of political parties in Thailand shortly thereafter, there has been a tendency for leadership of these irredentist movements to be external rather than internal. It is reported that certain extremist political parties in Malaysia, particularly some based in the east coast states, have been more or less constantly agitating within Pattani, Yala, and Narathiwat for a separation from Thailand. This situation is somewhat harder for the Thai government to deal with effectively, as it involves citizens and organizations of Malaysia, a country with which Thailand maintains (on most levels) extremely close and friendly relations.

Aware that stability gained by military repression is temporary at best, and with the added complication of external leadership, the present trend of the Thai government has been to treat the dissatisfactions of the Malays as constructively as possible. That is, legitimate demands of this group are usually being met insofar as this is consistent with the over-all goal of integration of all the citizens of the kingdom. As some government officials have recently put it, "we must match Malaya" in all those areas where the Malays of Thailand now make comparisons that find Thailand wanting. Once guidelines for constructive policy had been established in Bangkok, local Malay leadership became available both for its implementation and for the necessary job of selling it to the village population. These are the leaders of the second type mentioned above who accept the goal of ultimate integration as part of Thailand and who within this framework, are striving for fair treatment of the Malays in the area and for the Malays' full enjoyment of the fruits of Thai citizenship.

The area that has received the most attention in this connection is education, for this can both satisfy demands for education itself on the part of the people, and can also, through instruction in the Thai language, serve the ultimate end of integration. In addition to attempting to increase the span of compulsory primary school attendance from four to seven years, the government is committed to a program of increasing the number of schools in the South by twenty-five a year. Vocational schools have been established in all the capital towns and in some of the smaller towns in these provinces as well. Four teacher training institutes have recently been established in the Malay-speaking provinces and just outside. Mention has already been made of the work of the General Educational Development Centre in Yala in the area of language instruction and curriculum modification to meet the special needs of the South. It is in connection with this work that many educated Malays find scope for advancement in the civil service hierarchy. There has been persistent talk in Pattani and Yala about government plans to establish a University of the South in Pattani, and with sufficient pressure, the government may well match rumor with fact.[1]

Connected with developments in education is the government's policy on acceptance of religious differences among its citizens. Evidence of this policy has already been cited in the form of the mosque built by the government in Pattani, and by the inclusion in southern curricula of electives on the history of Islam (with de-emphasis of Buddhist morals). However, Muslims in South Thailand fear that this religious toleration may be more apparent than real, pointing to eventual government plans to abolish the Islamic religious schools in the area, substituting for them further electives in Islamic history in the government secondary schools. Meanwhile, the *pondok* are functioning to further the government's aims of spreading the knowledge of Thai (there is one *pondok* for every three primary schools in this area), and it is doubtful that this function will soon be sacrificed.

It is expected that the community development and resettlement programs will have a growing impact on the area. Even if their explicit goals of increasing productivity and living standards in general are not fully realized, they are having the effect of bringing to the area a relatively large number of Thai persons on a permanent basis. These Thais are both peasant cultivators in the settlement projects and educated, functional civil servants. It is inevitable that their increasing numbers will have a direct effect on the Malays. The field of public health and medicine is another in which progress has been made. Government hospitals in the capital towns are fairly good and staffed with competent Thai doctors, who, although they are civil servants, are generally more permanent residents of the area than their administrative counterparts. A training center for assistant nurses is operating at Narathiwat, and some training in simple nursing is given to Malay girls by the missionary hospital at Saiburi. A regular nursing school is planned for Songkhla, just outside the Malay-speaking area. Although DDT spraying campaigns have reduced the death rate from malaria from 250 per hundred thousand in 1949 to seventeen in 1963, much is still needed in the way of public health measures. Tuberculosis, leprosy, and filaria are serious problems in the South to which the government, with the assistance of the World Health Organization, is addressing itself. Yaws has been controlled but its widespread eradication is not in sight. Wide incidence of gonorrhea and typhoid fever has received little or no attention under public health programs. Essential public health work and improvement of general medical and

---

[1] Construction of the University of the South is scheduled to begin early in 1966. The site is just on the outskirts of Rusembilan village.

nursing facilities will, like the economic development programs, bring increased numbers of well-motivated Thais into contact with the Malay villager, with the probable result of facilitating integration.

While the possibility of Communist activities in South Thailand has existed at least since the early stages of World War II, it has not been until recently that the government recognized this possibility as a serious threat with far-reaching international implications (see Warner 1965:32) During the war, organized groups of guerrillas opposing the Japanese occupation of Malaya were active on both sides of the frontier. Leadership and much of the membership of these groups was Chinese, but because the groups contained Malayan Malays and were fighting to wrest Malaya from Japanese invaders, the majority of villagers in South Thailand were sympathetic. This sympathy was shown by providing food, rest, and shelter to the guerrillas in those areas near the frontier. With the cessation of hostilities, the return of the British to Malaya, and the new-formed friendship between Britain and Thailand, the guerrilla activity continued, but South Thai sympathy waned. No longer were these groups fighting to liberate Malaya from an invader, they were now fighting to overthrow a Malayan order which promised to be (and became) a Malayan nation. Needless to say, the guerrilla groups lost most of their Malay members. During the Malayan emergency, lasting until independence in 1957, these groups, frankly Communist-inspired, battled against British and Malayan troops within the Federation, and again sought food and refuge in the jungles of South Thailand. This aid now had to be achieved by threat or actual violence. The villagers of interior South Thailand had little recourse, as police protection did not extend far from the district headquarters, and treaty agreements forbade Thailand from sending regular military units into the border area. Villagers, remembering occasions when they were forced to pay Thais protection money, now reluctantly paid for protection to Communist guerrillas.

There is anxiety in Bangkok that Malay dissatisfaction with some government policies may be strong enough to induce elements of the population in South Thailand to support this Communist activity. However, it is unlikely that the Malay population will manifest its dissatisfaction by supporting groups who avow the destruction of Malaysia. At present the positive attraction of identification as Malays with a progressive Malaysian nation seems to be significantly stronger than the negative feelings toward Thai rule, particularly as at least the educated Malays in Thailand recognize the progressive direction some recent government policy is taking.

What does all this mean for the villager of Rusembilan and the half a million or so villagers like him throughout South Thailand? It means, first of all, that he will have greater contact with government officials than he had in the past. Probably he will find this contact somewhat less oppressive than before. He will certainly find more fellow Malays in positions of authority. More secular education is bound to affect every village child, and it is probable that efforts to teach the Thai language will ultimately be effective (in Satun, less isolated from government centers, the use of Thai is almost universal). With the requisite language skills, more and more Malay children will receive education beyond the primary level, and thus have opened to them employment opportunities (mostly in the civil service) unavailable to all but a few Malays today. Technical assistance will increasingly find its way into the area, improving many traditional occupational opportunities. It is likely that village fishing, already undergoing change, will change in the direction of larger scale operations more efficiently managed, so that an increasing number of people in coastal villages will not be able to pursue this as a full-time vocation. This in turn will continue to undermine the village social organizations built upon successful fishing careers. As these villages are organized today, this can only mean a further decline in the status and authority of the *orang baik* and a corresponding ascendancy of religious leaders as arbiters of village values and leaders in community affairs. The position of the religious leaders in the village will probably also be strengthened by the encroachment of government education outside of the village. No longer will the *pondok* (if they are ultimately allowed to exist at all) serve to train a large proportion of village youths in Islam; religious training will largely be concentrated in the hands of local Imams and village religious leaders. They will function as both *gurus* and as religious practitioners. In short, if the Royal Thai government pursues consistently the policies and programs it has established in the South, it will probably, within a generation, achieve the goal it has set for itself: creation in the South of full citizens of the Kingdom of Thailand, no longer Malays resident in Thailand, but Muslim Thais.

Glossary

abang: Elder brother, also applied to friends on the speaker's own generation who are older than he is.

adek: Younger brother, younger sister, also applied to close friends on the speaker's own generation who are younger than he is.

akikah: A ceremony, involving the ritual shaving of a child's head, at which a child is formally given his name.

amphur: In Thailand, the district or administrative unit beneath the province. *Nai Amphur:* The district officer.

anak: Child.

Ashura: Islamic celebration corresponding to the Day of Atonement.

atap: Roof thatching material made out of palm leaves.

awang: Son, also applied familiarly to other male children.

bagian: Share or portion. *bagian besar:* System of fish distribution in which ordinary crewmen are entitled to one large share. *bagian ketchil:* Fish distribution system involving twice as many small shares as above, but avoiding fractional shares.

baht: Thai currency unit, equivalent to approximately 5 cents.

baik: Morally good. *orang baik:* A morally good man, applied to respected leaders of the community.

balaisa: Chapel. In Rusembilan, it is a secondary religious structure which, because of its location is of greater social significance than the *surau* or village mosque.

bapa: Father; see also *pak*.

bidan: Midwife, usually with limited shamanistic powers.

bomo: Shaman or curer employing both herbal and spiritualistic techniques.

changwat: In Thailand, the province; the largest administrative unit below the nation in modern Thailand.

dike ulu: A competitive singing contest in which one individual or team attempts to best the other with humorous or derogatory verses.

durian: A large, strong-smelling fruit, popular in much of Southeast Asia. It is often grown as an adjunct to rubber.

guru: A teacher, specifically religious.

gurah: A bullock-pulled rake used to smooth the rice fields after heavy plowing with the *nanga*.

hantu: Traditional malevolent spirits. *Hantu Niyam:* A particular spirit who tries to enter the womb of a postpartem mother, causing harm to both her and her infant.

Hari Raya: Great day or feast day; specifically, *Hari Raya Haji:* celebrating a pilgrimage to Mecca, and *Hari Raya Puasa:* celebrating the end of the fasting month.

Hukim: Islamic law, in contrast to traditional or secular law.

Imam: Islamic priest, leader of the religious congregation.

jin or *jin Islam:* Spirits of Islamic origin in contrast to traditional *hantu.*

jokung: A small, often crudely made boat, used extensively for fishing by one or two persons close to shore.

kadi: A judge; here, specifically versed in *Hukim.*

kakak: Elder sister.

kamnan: The Thai official governing the *tambon,* or group of villages, directly under the *amphur* in the admistrative hierarchy.

kampong: A village or community.

kedai kopi: Literally, coffee shop; foci for congregation in Malay villages where tea is served and a small variety of staples are sold.

kembong: Mackerel, the most important species of fish caught by village fishermen of South Thailand.

kolek: A boat, 35–50 feet in length, used for fishing in offshore waters.

latah: A form of mental disease involving mimetic speech and behavior.

machu: "Aunt" used in address, also applied as a term of respect to women of an older generation.

Majalis Ugama: Religious board; a Muslim group advisory to the provincial government which also supervises local religious affairs.

mak: Mother, also applied to women of an older generation as a term more respectful than *machu.* Term of reference for "aunt" when used with the appropriate term for age relative to the connecting relative: *lung* (older), *ngah* (middle), *su* (younger).

makan: Eat; *makan nasi:* to eat rice or, simply, to eat a meal; *makan pulot:* to eat glutenous rice or, by extension, any feast where this type of rice is appropriate.

masjid: Mosque.

Masuk Jawi: The ceremony celebrating a boy's puberty, literally, entering Malay-hood.

Maulud: Celebration of the birth of the Prophet Mohammed.

me: Daughter, also applied familiarly to other female children.

murid: Religious student.

mutu: Motor launch; *mutu Imam:* the motor launch purchased by the Imam of Rusembilan.

naiban: South Thai term for the elected head of the village or *muban.*

nanga: A bullock-drawn plow used for the first breaking of the ground before planting rice.

nasi: Rice which has been prepared for eating. *nasi semangat:* rice prepared for certain ceremonies containing special quantities of *semangat,* soul-stuff or vital force.

orang: Man. *orang baik:* A morally good man, applied to traditional village leaders.

pachu: "Uncle" used in address, also applied as a term of respect to men of an older generation.

padi: Unprocessed rice or rice growing in the field.

pak: Father, also applied to men of an older generation as a term more respectful than *pachu.* Term of reference for "uncle" when used with the appropriate term for age relative to the connecting relative: *lung* (older), *ngah* (middle), *su* (younger).

parang: A common knife with broad hooked end, 18 inches to 2 feet in length.

pelesit: A familiar spirit.

perabu: Boat in general. Correctly, the term should be applied in speaking of any boat, as in *perabu kolek.*

petai: The long, "bean"-filled pod, growing on certain jungle trees, eaten on occasion by Malay villagers.

peterana: A play performed by spirits through the medium of the *bomo* and others for the enjoyment of the spirits.

pondok: A Muslim religious school which boys may attend after completing village religious instruction.

rai: Thai unit of areal measurement—about $2\frac{1}{2}$ *rai* make an acre.

rambutan: A jungle fruit about the size of a lemon whose grapelike interior is covered with a hairy red rind.

sapupu: "Cousin" in exactly the same sense as in English.

sarong: Sheath or tube; *kain sarong* is the sheathlike clothing characteristically worn as a lower garment by Malay men and women.

saudara: Relative; *anak saudara:* a term applied to nieces and nephews.

sawahnillo: A tree-borne, caramelly, brown-skinned fruit.

semangat: Soul-stuff, mana or vital force, resident in different degrees in all things.

sembayang: Prayer. *sembayang hajat:* A special afternoon prayer of petition.

silat: A stylized dance and mock fight performed for the amusement of spirits.

surau: A building for religious congregation and service which does not meet the standards for a true mosque, or *masjid.*

tambon: Thai term for commune or group of villages under the leadership of the *kamnan.*

tok: Grandfather or grandmother, also applied as a term of respect to elderly persons, or to highly respected persons of less advanced age.

ubi: Edible tuber; *ubi kayu:* sweet manioc; *ubi keladi:* taro.

udang: Prawn or shrimp; *udang ako:* large prawn; *udang belachan:* very small shrimp, salted and ground into a paste.

wayong kulit: Traditional shadow play, formerly performed for the amusement of spirits.

wak: Old man, a term of modest respect for an elderly individual who is not entitled to other respect terms.

zakat: Annual religious tithe.

References Cited

ANONYMOUS, ca. 1952, *Annals of Pattani* (in Malay). Pattani, Thailand: privately published.

FRASER, T. M., 1960, *Rusembilan: A Malay Fishing Village in Southern Thailand*. Ithaca, N.Y.: Cornell University Press.

KROEBER, A. L., 1948, *Anthropology*. New York: Harcourt, Brace & World, Inc.

NEWBOLD, T. J., 1839, *Political and Statistical Account of the British Settlements in the Straits of Malacca*. (2 vols.) London: J. Murray.

WARNER, D., 1965, "Thailand: Peking's New Front." *The Reporter,* June 17, pp. 32–34.

Recommended Reading

Southeast Asia—General

DOBBY, E. H. G., 1960, *Southeast Asia* (7th ed). London: University of London Press.

A standard geography of Southeast Asia. Especially good for Malaya and, by extension, the Malay-speaking provinces of South Thailand.

HALL, D. G. E., 1955, *A History of South-east Asia*. New York: St. Martin's Press.

A comprehensive history of Southeast Asia. Includes material on the northern Malay kingdoms which is not readily available in other general works.

LEBAR, F. M., G. C. HICKEY, and J. K. MUSGRAVE, 1964, *Ethnic Groups of Mainland Southeast Asia*. New Haven, Conn.: Human Relations Area Files Press.

The standard ethnographic reference on mainland Southeast Asia. Section on Malays contains data on Malays of South Thailand and comparisons with those of Malaysia.

Political Setting

THOMPSON, V., and R. ADLOFF, 1955, *Minority Problems in Southeast Asia.* Stanford, Calif.: Stanford University Press.

Contains a short section dealing with the position of the Malay "minority" in South Thailand. The Chinese of Thailand and Malaya are also briefly treated.

WILSON, D. A., 1962, *Politics in Thailand.* Ithaca, N.Y.: Cornell University Press.

A perceptive, up-to-date account of the political system and power structure of Thailand. There is no specific reference to problems of South Thailand, but the total political context provides valuable background.

Cultural Studies

FIRTH, RAYMOND, 1946, *Malay Fishermen: Their Peasant Economy.* London: Routledge and Kegan Paul.

A classic anthropological account of village fishing economies of Kelantan and Trengganu. These villagers are similar in many respects to fishermen of South Thailand.

FIRTH, ROSEMARY, 1943, *Housekeeping among Malay Peasants.* (London School of Economics, Monographs on Social Anthropology No. 7.) London.

A study made at the same time as *Malay Fishermen,* stressing domestic economy and the village woman's role in coastal Malay society.

FRASER, T. M., 1960, *Rusembilan: A Malay Village in Southern Thailand.* Ithaca, N.Y.: Cornell University Press.

The only monograph dealing specifically with the Malays of South Thailand. This is the full ethnographic account of Rusembilan in 1956, providing many cultural details which could not be presented in the present work.

WINSTEDT, R. O., 1951, *The Malay Magician: Being Shaman, Saiva, and Sufi.* London: Routledge and Kegan Paul.

An analysis of traditional Malay beliefs and practices in regard to the supernatural. Isolates animistic, Hindu, and Muslim aspects.

————, 1953, *The Malays: A Cultural History.* London: Routledge and Kegan Paul.

A general account of Malay culture. Considers a range of areal types as well as levels of society.